TILL DEATH US DO PART SCRIPTS

LONDON BBC Radio London
9–15 September 1972 Price 5p

BBC1 New Season:1

RadioTimes

Alf Garnett's back
Christening his grandson in Till Death Us Do Part
Wednesday BBC1 Colour
INSIDE: The Johnny Speight story

TILL DEATH DO PART SCRIPTS

Written by
JOHNNY SPEIGHT

Produced by
DENNIS MAIN WILSON

Illustrated by
STANLEY FRANKLIN

THE WOBURN PRESS

First published in Great Britain in 1973 by
THE WOBURN PRESS
67 Great Russell Street, London WC1B 3BT

Copyright © 1973 Johnny Speight

ISBN 0 7130 0086 7

The publishers acknowledge with thanks the
co-operation of the BBC

Acknowledgements
are due to Mr Carl Giles for his cartoon
The Radio Times Hulton Picture Library (for photographs of
Garnett family with Johnny Speight and of Anthony Booth)
BBC Pictorial Publicity Department (for photograph of Garnett family)

Radio Times (for permission to reproduce
the front cover, of Garnett family Christening)
The Observer (for George Melly's extract)
Evening Standard (for Milton Shulman's extract)
News of the World (for Graham Stanford's extract)
The Guardian (for Stanley Reynold's extract)
Daily Mirror (for extract)
The Spectator (for extract)
New Statesman and Mr Malcolm Muggeridge
(for Malcolm Muggeridge's extract)
Financial Times (for T.C. Worsley's extract)
The Stage and Television Today (for extract)
Associated Newspaper Group Ltd.
(for Peter Black's extract from the *Daily Mail*)
The Times (for extract from third leading article)
The Listener and Mr Karl Miller (for Karl Miller's extract)

*All rights reserved. No part of this publication may be reproduced,
stored in a retrieval system, or transmitted in any form or by any
means, electronic, mechanical, photocopying, recording, or otherwise,
without the prior permission of The Woburn Press.*

Designed for the Woburn Press by Harold King
Printed in Great Britain by C. J. Mason & Sons Ltd.
Bristol BS13 7TP

Contents

Foreword by Dennis Main Wilson	11
Till Death Us Do Part...What the Papers Said	13
...And What They Said About Alf Garnett	14
The Writer, The Cast and The Cartoonist	16

The Scripts

The Bird Fancier	23
I can give it up anytime I like...	43
Sex before Marriage	59
The Funeral	81
Women's Lib and Bournemouth	103
If we want a proper democracy we've got to start shooting a few people...	125
Royal Variety Performance 1972	147

Publisher's Note

These scripts were televised between 1966 and 1972. With the invaluable and endlessly patient assistance of Johnny Speight, Dennis Main Wilson and Stanley Franklin, we have translated them to the printed page, where they will no doubt continue to amuse, appal and infuriate, and remind us of the Garnett family – and ourselves.

Stanley Franklin's cartoons have been drawn specially for the book; apart from these, we felt the scripts required no additions – the members of the Garnett family speak for themselves on subjects with which we are now all familiar, and which they deal with in their inimitable style.

The scripts have been faithfully reproduced; sufficient stage directions have been left in to make sense of a script transferred from a visual to a written medium. Johnny Speight would be particularly pleased if the book was used by amateur dramatic groups around the country.

'Till Death Us Do Part' is now famous inside and outside Britain. It is the top T.V. show in Britain itself, it is being shown in America, Holland, Germany and is planned for other countries. It has achieved every sort of fame and notoriety in high and low places. We hope that this transplant from the screen to the page has been successful.

Foreword
Dennis Main Wilson

Since we started in 1966, "Till Death Us Do Part" has been praised as "magnificent comic realism" – attacked as "obscene filth" – Commanded to appear before Royalty – and Apologised for by Authority.

Consistently rated the top T.V. comedy show in Britain, the Americanised version "All In The Family" the best comedy series in the U.S.A., top show in Australia, it is now being produced in Holland and Germany.

And yet "Till Death Us Do Part" never began as grandly as that. I had admired Johnny Speight's work for a long time – from the Arthur Haynes sketch shows for ATV – to the *serious* plays he had written for my Aunt the BBC, and it frustrated me that he wasn't writing *comedy* for the BBC – because his serious plays were very funny.

My Aunt the BBC by the way was, and still is, an extremely ethical old lady with whom I have enjoyed an incredibly incestuous relationship for years. Only she would have had the nerve to hoist her skirts, throw away her chastity belt – and originate the most controversial T.V. series ever.

In 1964, Speight and I found that we both sought a form of comedy which would truthfully depict the shambles that Homo Sapiens has made out of what God created in those six days (or what evolution created in a rather longer time).

We began to enthuse – it took two years of intense alcoholic endeavour. Remember the Great Whisky drought of 1964 – '65? That was us.

I commissioned Johnny to write a script for an experimental "Comedy Playhouse" series that I was producing. He eventually brought in five pages of Cockney dialogue – no plot – just the dialogue. It only ran about three minutes – but the quality of the writing was unmistakably brilliant. Johnny finished the script – I cast the performers and we made the pilot show. It wasn't bad – certainly the Press hailed it. One London critic – Peter Black – thundered "Don't make it a series. Repeat *this* one four times a year!" My Aunt the BBC, on the other hand, muttered something about "over her corporate dead body" but, ethical old lady that she is, offered us a series.

Foreword

The rest is common knowledge. "Alf Garnett" has become a household name – Speight has developed into a writer of international repute, almost in spite of the fact that "Till Death Us Do Part" failed in its primary objective. Our intention was to hold a mirror up to the world. Let it see itself – warts and all. Garnett was to be put in the pillory of public shame. With his loud-mouthed bigotries he was to be the anti-hero. He was to be laughed *at* – not *with*.

It didn't really work out that way. A few people sensed what we were up to. The majority just enjoyed the show and missed the point.

A minority were outraged by Speight's scorn for the Establishment (*any* Establishment), by his broadsides against compartmentalized religion and by his utter contempt for that conspiracy of mediocrity which accompanies the advance of "civilisation" – a dire disease from which the human race seems destined to die.

That it didn't work out as planned is no surprise really. When we started "Till Death" Speight was a self-proclaimed Socialist – and you know what *they're* like. Over the years, however, as Speight has knocked man-made Christianity, he's probably begun to spot the same human defects in man-made Socialism too. He certainly feels that Capitalism brings out the efficient worst in human nature – he's probably aware too that Socialism brings out its inefficient, bureaucratic best.

I am firmly of the opinion that Johnny Speight now sees neither hope nor comfort for mankind in any current "–isms" whatsoever. He's even given up drinking, the swine – and you know what that can do to a man – no faith in anything!

The only clue to his new, teetotal state of mind is that he now acknowledges a Power greater than all of us (I hope to God it's not Garnett) and that there *is* some kind of order in all our current disorders.

I sense that Speight is observing this world as if it's inside a great goldfish bowl – watching and waiting to write about what happens next. I also sense that both Speight and his goldfish bowl are inside another, even bigger goldfish bowl – and that there's another Bloke outside *that* one . . . watching and waiting . . .

I hope I'm there to produce it when it happens . . . with my Aunt, of course.

Dennis Main Wilson 1973.

What the Papers Said

'Johnny Speight's scripts revealed a shocking lot of people in a household where politics is a matter of mindless catch-phrases and argument means crushing by insult. Mrs. Garnett emerged from stupor only to exult over her husband's misfortunes. Their comparatively inoffensive daughter existed only in a sort of mindless sexuality.

Mike, her irresponsible but progressive mate, is as appalling a subject for consideration as Alf himself, and if the series had gone on much longer, Alf's racial prejudices, his coarseness, his cowardice, and his combination of bullying arrogance with toadying servility would have attracted, it seems, as much critical comment and exegesis as *Hamlet*. Of course, it was all beautifully acted; who would have missed the sight of Dandy Nichols wakening from torpor to malicious derision, or the exquisite timing of her more obtuse remarks? And the greatest compliment to Warren Mitchell is to note that he has become a real nightmare, though not very long ago he was only a sympathetic, sensitive actor.

The objection to *Till Death Us Do Part* is not that it is a malicious, lying attack on the English race, but that, alas, it is terribly true. Lives like that are led; marriages as sour as that of Alf and Else exist. There are those who toady to any authority, while announcing that, like other Britons, they never will be slaves, whose patriotism ineffectively disguises dread of the unknown, and terrified resentment of the new.

Irony has never gone down well in England. Therefore, Mr. Speight must, some of us are convinced, approve of Alf or else of Mike, otherwise he would not have locked them in ludicrous combat. Alf Garnett is a monster, created with obvious delight, but *Till Death Us Do Part* is a justifiably angry outcry against the poverty of mind and spirit in which vast numbers of people spend their lives. Yet so ambivalent is irony and our response to irony that Alf Garnett's preposterous prejudices seemed also at times a welcome relief from the relentless drip of official liberalism on the B.B.C.'

The Times, 17 February 1968

'The most successful of this season's *Comedy Playhouse* was Johnny Speight's *Till Death Us Do Part*, which took me into a solitary purple haze of laughter.

The awful family he created must not die with but one performance.'

Peter Black, *Daily Mail*, 20 August 1965

'From its beginning, Till Death introduced a vigorous new element into television comedy. It did not rely on jokes or funny situations but on the extreme attitudes and prejudices of its central character. Alf Garnett was a loud-mouthed bigot and reactionary, and the very antithesis of the enlightened attitudes that are currently *de rigueur*. Although he was superficially a working-class character. Alf's brand of bigotry and dogmatism can be found anywhere. It was with these recognisable, far from humorous, and exaggerated failings that Johnny Speight attacked unthinking acceptance of many of our society's standards and establishments. Somewhere, sometime, we have all heard one of Alf Garnett's tirades and have come away feeling smug about our own liberalism.

Such a programme, with its vigorous realism of language, was certain to arouse the anger of those who, perhaps unconsciously, want to impose their own morality on viewers.'

The Stage and Television Today, 22 February 1968

'No programme has ever commanded such hearty laughter and shocked condemnation, such sheer delight and superior scorn. No vehicle of public comment has been so courageous in dealing with racial issues, party politics, sex and society.

For the first time in television history, Britain has a skilfully written, impeccably acted series dealing with serious political issues by sending them up as high as possible.'

Reading Evening Post, 4 April 1967

'It is magnificent comic realism, with fine acting performances—Dandy Nichols is fit to wear a crown of her own. Johnny Speight has created a household name—I wonder if the complainers have any idea of how much this means.'

Karl Miller, *The Listener*, 22 February 1968

And What They Said About Alf Garnett

'Mr Speight seems to me to be one of the best comic writers of the day... Already, with his sketches for the late Arthur Haynes, Mr. Speight was showing us what he was going to be capable of...

What was original about his approach was the positively breathtaking rudeness which he injected into his characterisation of the tramp...

Something of a similar extremity and excess – of an almost sacriligious effrontery – is what characterises Alf Garnett of *Till Death Us Do Part*, the finest flower of Mr. Speight's invention so far. Alf Garnett is a positively Falstaffian figure in its size and impact. If, instead of appearing in this transient medium, he had been the central figure of a stage comedy, he would instantly have been recognised as a major comic creation to be discussed and re-visited and revived over and over again... The series is the nearest equivalent on television to the stage play, slowly developing a character over the weeks, unfolding more and more of him, as a play does over an evening...

Who, then, is this Alf Garnett and what is he? Why, he is the rampaging, howling embodiment of all the most vulgar and odious prejudices that slop about in the bilges of the national mind. Whatever hidden hates, irrational fears and superseded loyalties stand in the way of our slow stumble towards a more civilised society, Alf Garnett is the living, blaspheming expression of them. He is everything most hateful about our national character – xenophobic, illiberal, racist, anti-semitic, toadying, authoritarian. He's a flogger, a hanger, a censor, a know-all and a Mister-Always-Right. He is a positive anthology of unconsidered bigotry.

How is it then, you may ask, if he is so despicable, that Mr. Speight manages to make of him something so appealing as well as so funny? But isn't just this the peculiar virtue of the comic genius that it at the same time exposes vices to our laughter and allows us to love the creatures who embody those vices? Maddening though it must be fore Mrs. Whitehouse, the more cowardly, bragging and dishonourable Falstaff is, the more we love him. It is the same with Alf Garnett. The more outrageous and extreme his tirades grow, the more we adore him. But make no mistake, we don't admire him, not in the least. We laugh not with him, but at him.

... In Alf Garnett, Mr. Speight brings out fully into the light of day all the absurdity and irrationality of prejudices that even the most enlightened of us probably harbour somewhere in the sink-pipe of our minds. But bring them out into the open-air, and we see them for what they really are...

This is the public service that Mr. Speight is performing – cleansing the Augean stable of our national vices of mind. And it wouldn't be as effective as it is if Alf Garnett were not the wholly outrageous figure of Mr. Speight's invention. It's no use complaining that he is offensive. He is, indeed, just as completely offensive as everything he embodies is offensive. The one exposes the other. And it takes some audacity of mind to make him so extreme as he is. That is Mr. Speight's special quality – that audacity of mind which is prepared to go further than any of us would dare to go.

It is in his tirades, his superb flow of uninhibited invective, that Alf Garnett really reveals himself. They are the special point of the series, they are what we wait for and treasure...'

T. C. Worsley, *Financial Times*

'The fascination of Alf Garnett, the monstrous hero of the BBC's *Till Death Us Do Part*, lay in his ability to act as a distorting mirror in which we could watch our meanest attributes reflected large and ugly.

Like some boil on the back of the neck that one cannot resist stroking or touching, this social aberration demanded the nation's attention.

Some 18 million viewers—half of Britain's adult population—watched him weekly wallowing in the hates and fears and prejudices most of us have tucked away in some genteel niche of our psyche.

Alf's views on coons, kikes and wogs; his reflections on Labour Party politicians; his suspicion of anything new like transplant operations; his ignorant superstitions, his insensitivity to beauty, his blatant hypocrisy can be seen and heard most days in most pubs, factories and boardrooms in the land.

Even his conventional virtues—his faith, his patriotism, his loyalties—have all been acquired for the wrong reasons. His religion is motivated by fear of a vengeful God; his admiration of the Queen, by snobbery; his passion for West Ham, by a need for aggressive self-fulfilment.

The difference between Alf and most of us is that he brandishes his decadent and violent ideas in the foul-mouthed linguistic setting that suited them best. He was too uncultivated and ignorant to realise that if he disguised them under a veneer of propriety, they would have been acceptable in some of our best drawing-rooms.'

Milton Shulman,
Evening Standard,
21 February 1968

'He was officially defensible only, it seems, if he were a monster. The programme's chief critics seemed only pleased if Garnett was done down each week. He had to be left out of parties, snubbed, shown to be a coward, a liar, and a possible cheat. He could be forgiven his energy only if he possessed all the other bad characteristics that those in power like to see in the working-classes. One had seen Alf Garnett as a character that G. K. Chesterton liked to call "the English poor" and that George Orwell liked to call "the English proletariat," but with a tongue in his mouth and the energy to wag it.

The people who could not stand Alf were invariably those who do not much care for any show of energy, especially from the classes who are safest when meek and mild. Certainly Alf was an Empire man, but his logic was so mixed up that he could hardly appeal to the viewing Empiremen. Let Alf Garnett slip once too often on his own mad logic and all that energy would be spent raising barricades; it best served the peace and calm of society if Alf remained merely foul-mouthed and blasphemous.

Before this last series he had been an Orwellian character with misplaced loyalties of Dickensian proportions.'

Stanley Reynolds, *The Guardian*, 17 February 1968

'... this Falstaff among programmes ... managed ... to contain general and universal truths within a particularised and temporal shell. By creating Alf Garnett and his wife, Johnny Speight has added two figures to the small pantheon of immortal comic monsters, the Père and Mère Ubu of the Welfare State, and in time this will appear to have been his great achievement.

But it has had a more didactic function. He probed, with an admirable contempt for our sensibilities, into the social sores and abscesses which we have tried to ignore in the vain hope that they might cure themselves. He is, in fact, a moralist and, like all true moralists, became the object of hatred and denigration to those who confuse morality with "good taste."'

George Melly, *The Observer*, 25 February 1968

'There's something of the awful Alf in all of us. Who could truly claim that we are entirely free of his bigotries, hypocrisies and acts of petty cowardice? And who could deny that even as we laugh at Alf we know deep down that in one way or another we share some of his outrageous prejudices?

This loud-mouthed, ranting, ignorant reactionary with his loathsome manners probed our conscience every Friday night.

Through Alf, the brilliant Speight exposed the pathetic futility of snobbery in all its forms. For Alf—vulgar, ignorant, greedy and selfish—was the arch-snob who became a subservient, cringing crawler in the presence of his "betters."'

Graham Stanford, *News of the World*, 18 February 1968

'As 10 to 14 million viewers well know, *Till Death Us Do Part* portrays what is supposed to be a typical contemporary working-class home and family. The main character is the father, Alf Garnett, a rampaging, stupid, opinionated old fellow in constant conflict with his with-it daughter and her long-haired husband, both of whom have been washed clean in the comprehensive streams and, unlike poor old Alf, sent out into the world enlightened and purified of unreason and prejudice—in fact, as good guys. There is also Mrs. Garnett, to me, I must say, the most tolerable of the grisly quartet, perhaps only because she spends a lot of her time dozing.

It is interesting that Alf, like Andy Capp, the *Daily Mirror* hero, is credited with working-class ways—such as sitting about in his braces—which have long since been obsolete, and belong nowadays more to the telly—especially the drama department—than to life. Maybe the good-guy/bad-guy legend requires pasteboard proletarians, as it does pasteboard gentry, to sustain itself. Alf, in any case, is the bad guy incarnate, and expresses at the top of his voice all the deplorable attitudes that go therewith—down with the wogs! bring back the hangman! no pre-marital sex! send the niggers home and the buggers to prison! good old Smithy! it's all a Red plot! etc. etc.

We are expected to laugh contemptuously at this wild old reprobate and buffoon, contrasting with his grotesque obscurantism the good-guy attitudes of the young people—Americans have outstayed their welcome in Vietnam, sex is good and the *Chatterley*-Comfort rules are a better guide to its enjoyment than the *Book of Common Prayer*, the Bolshies are human, too, the good life is just round the corner and we'll all get there once Alf and his like have disappeared from the scene for ever, and so on. Every swinging, swirling, trendy indication is that the young ones are in the right, and that shocking old Alf is a lone survivor from a vanished age, soon to be heard no more. There's the moral, plain as plain.

Yet here's the extraordinary thing—audience research and other personal impressions seem to indicate that, far from being the clown-villian of the series, Alf is the hero. His crazy outpourings ring the bell for millions of viewers; he's their hero, they dote on him and hang on his words.'

Malcolm Muggeridge, *New Statesman*, 15 December 1967

'No television character has sparked off such adjectival excesses as has this hairless malingerer with the distorted, hypocritical view of life, people, religion and Her Britannic Majesty.

"Brilliant," "Despicable," "Crude," "Perceptive," "Harmful," or "Timely," are sample comments taken from the large dossier on "Till Death Us Do Part."'

'Alf Garnett was compulsive watching for millions, even for those unfortunate ones who relished this confirmation of their own intolerance unable to see the parody behind prejudice.

Conceived by Johnny Speight it was "think" entertainment on a devastating level. Behind every belly laugh was the nagging thought: "is there a hint of Alf Garnett in me?"'

Daily Mirror, 8 August 1968

'No one could pretend that Alf is stoical but he has other Roman virtues, of a decadent Rome, maybe, with the Visigoths closing in, but clearly ones which have a considerable appeal to many in this country, principally a crude, ill-informed loyalty to the institutions that shadowed his early years.'

The Spectator, 21 October 1972

The Writer, The Cast and The Cartoonist

Johnny Speight on the set of Till Death Us Do Part with the cast.

JOHNNY SPEIGHT

JOHNNY SPEIGHT *is married and has three children. His relaxation is watching West Ham. He was born in London's Canning Town, the son of a docker.*

'I left school at 14 after being educated to be a factory worker. I mean that. Factory workers was what the school thought they were turning out.'

The war proved to be a turning point:

'Really I didn't come alive till entered the army. I was hardly conscious of the world around me until then. Living in Canning Town in those days was like being in prison, because unless you were a boxer or something like that your chances of getting out were very remote.'

He took up drumming and moved about in the West End with musicians and artists before beginning to write.

'One afternoon I was in Canning Town Public Library looking for a book and I came across one by George Bernard Shaw. At that time Bernard Shaw was always being quoted in the papers, and I thought he was a comic like Tommy Trinder and that I ought to go and see him some time because I liked his wit. When I saw this book, I thought: 'Christ, he writes as well' . . . So I took it home and read it from cover to cover . . . And from that day I was completely hooked. And I decided that I wanted to be a writer, too.'

His first break into writing comedy came when he was introduced to Frankie Howerd, who liked some of his material and suggested that he meet Eric Sykes. From Sykes he met Spike Milligan, and Simpson and Galton, and they found him a job writing some links for an Edmundo Ros radio programme. From there he went to working with Morecambe and Wise, and then to Arthur Haynes, for whom he wrote something like 500 scripts. It was in the early sixties that he created the figure of Alf Garnett. He has written two stage plays – **The Knacker's Yard,** *put on at the Arts Theatre Club, where it was censored, and the award-winning* **If There Weren't Any Blacks . . . You'd Have To Invent Them;** *he has also written several plays for television – among others,* **The Playmates, The Compartment** *and* **The Salesman.** *And of course there's* **Curry and Chips,** *another controversial television series . . .*

WARREN MITCHELL

WARREN MITCHELL (*real name Misell* – 'I changed it during a stint of disc jockeying on Radio Luxembourg – they said the spelling was too difficult for people sending in requests') *was born in Stoke Newington. He is married to actress Constance Wake and has three children. In his spare time he plays clarinet in a local wind ensemble.*
'My background is working class; I had the Cockney patter. I was eager for learning, wanted to make something of my life. I think, too, I was keen on improving my accent, for after only six months at Oxford (*University, where he studied physical chemistry*) there wasn't a trace of Cockney left. I was speaking the very frightfully stuff. I blush at the memory. 'Time we had a crack at the Hun, old boy,' I would say to my officer-cadet pals in the University Air Squadron.'
However, he was sailing to Canada to begin training as an aircrew navigator when Germany surrendered in 1945.
'One of my buddies was Richard Burton. . . It was Burton, really, who gave me the urge to be an actor. After the war I went to RADA on a grant, then into the theatre (*London's little Unity Theatre* – 'that's where I properly discovered what acting was really all about').'

The name Warren Mitchell may not have been well known to the public, but it was to producers, who have long counted him among the most versatile and reliable of artists.
'I was sitting at home waiting for my agent to come up trumps on my behalf when the phone rang. It was Dennis Main Wilson. He went into a great spiel about this 'great style role'. It all sounded so well rehearsed. Obviously he had been hunting around and had already approached a dozen other actors to play Alf. I cut in and said, 'Dennis, I'll DO it.' He went on to explain the part in detail. 'It's fine, Dennis,' I said. 'I'm not working. I'll do it.''
When he read the first script, Mitchell wasn't exactly carried away with the dialogue.
'I thought, 'Not much in this.' Seemed pretty mundane sort of stuff. I honestly thought nothing very much would come of the series . . . I took a second read at the script, and during rehearsals I began to catch a glimpse of the genius of this chap Speight. Mundane situations, yes . . . but what he did with them was something else . . . something great. Alf was coming through to me.'

THE PROGRAMME
'I'm all for the bold, bald truth in everything on TV. If you tone down Cockney outspokenness it goes all prissy.'
'I've always felt strongly about racialism. As a Jew I've always been aware of racial prejudice. *Till Death* makes the lunacy of racialism so much more apparent.'
'It's hard to change people's attitudes and expose their prejudices by lectures or pamphlets, but make them laugh and you make them think.'

ALF GARNETT
'That ignorant pig thinks he has his wife in complete subjugation. Else knows differently . . . she is like a seal. Alf's blusterings just run off her like water. She's inured to them.'
'I have come to hate the character to the point where I have to swallow hard before I can make him speak. I know it is brilliant writing, truthful and perceptive. I know that the whole point is to mirror the ugly prejudices in people. But I'm the one who has to do it. It is no joke. People tend to identify you with the character. One chap came over to me saying, 'I'm glad you had a go at the Queen and the coloureds.' I told him, 'You stupid so-and-so, I was having a go at you!' He looked quite stupified. This sort of thing worried me. Garnett was developing into a lovable sort of rogue. And the more popular he became, the more he offended me . . . the awful chauvinism of the man was beginning to wear me down. And his drunkenness and 'all-women-are-rubbish' stuff is a joke that needs a pretty strong stomach to play indefinitely.'

DANDY NICHOLS

DANDY NICHOLS, *widely praised for her generous, understated performance as the torpid, put-upon consort of the dreadful Alf.*

'I'm not a Cockney – I was born in Hammersmith. Including my parents, there were seven of us at home – but it wasn't half as noisy as the Garnett's. I didn't come from a stage background. Dad was an engineer. But I have been interested in acting since I was eight.'

Miss Nichols worked as a secretary in a London boot polish factory for twelve years. In her spare time she acted with the local dramatic society.

'A producer saw me and offered me a part in repertory. I grabbed it. I was a pound a week worse off – everybody thought I was mad. I didn't care – I was among the bright lights and grease paint. That was more than thirty years ago.'

Her first film was **Nicholas Nickleby** *in 1945; more recent films have been* **The Knack** *and* **The Early Bird.** *She has also appeared in many television series, including* **Emergency Ward 10, Dixon of Dock Green, Mrs Thursday, No Hiding Place** *and* **Here's Harry.**

THE PROGRAMME

'I know it's a bit outrageous at times, but I believe in sacred cows being knocked occasionally. It's the way it's said, not what is said, that matters.'

ELSE GARNETT

'A bit of an old slag. Not dirty but certainly not houseproud! A cabbage, not very much up top, obviously. Terrible antagonism between her and her husband, not much love lost. A very satisfying part, wonderfully observed by Johnny Speight. It was clever of him to think of Silly Old Moo. Other terms of abuse would have been more unpleasant and less memorable . . . Oh, yes, of course, I get Silly Old Moo shouted after me in the street. I've only got to wait at a bus stop for someone to start yelling and pointing . . . I could live without being called silly old moo by perfect strangers . . . By the way, I was really christened Daisy. Dandy is a throwback to my schooldays. I hated Daisy – it always reminded me of a cow.'

'I think Else over the years has become used to Alf, like the sound of the Underground at the bottom of the garden. In time you don't hear the noise it makes.'

ANTHONY BOOTH

ANTHONY BOOTH *left school at sixteen and spent a season with the Liverpool Playhouse. Then he went to sea for six months, returned to acting all over the provinces, and eventually reached London, where, in between spells as a Covent Garden porter, he broke into TV. His first big part was in* **Pay Day** *in 1960, the year in which he made his film debut in* **Suspect.** *He had been acting for ten years when Johnny Speight wrote the original* **Till Death Us Do Part** *play for Comedy Playhouse in 1965. A great friend of Johnny Speight, Mr Booth enjoys arguing for hours in his company, and thinks he's a fine writer whose only fault is* 'a hate against long hair on men'. *As for Alf:* 'By God, I hate Alf Garnett. Seriously. I just have to remember that I'm a pacifist, and that Warren isn't Alf Garnett.'

UNA STUBBS

UNA STUBBS *was born in Leicestershire. She became a chorus-girl at the London Palladium where she was known as Basher Stubbs because she showed off so much.* ('I was pathetic – I just wanted to be noticed.') *After her spell at the Palladium she did several TV commercials, and then got into* **Cool for Cats** *on television. She has worked for ten years with Cliff Richard, appearing with him in the films* **Summer Holiday** *and* **Wonderful Life,** *in pantomimes and a religious series in Newcastle, and in three of his television series. She recently played at the Mermaid Theatre for eight months in* **Cowardy Custard.** *In her fanmail she gets masses of sympathetic letters for living in that horrible Garnett household, but says* 'I feel very sorry for Alf Garnett – there really are a lot of people like him. He's so stubborn; you could never put any sense into his head. He's to be *pitied* more than anything. And it's so ghastly that Rita's married to someone like Mike, who doesn't work and won't help her to get out of the situation. And now that she's stuck with the baby, it's hopeless. She's becoming more and more like her mother – a block.'

STANLEY FRANKLIN

STANLEY FRANKLIN *was born in 1930. He studied drawing at the Mornington Crescent Working Men's College and Hammersmith School of Arts and Crafts. For fifteen years he worked as a freelance cartoonist in advertising; in 1959 he became political cartoonist of the London* Daily Mirror. *He left Fleet Street in 1970 to practise fine art. His ceramics and relief-paintings have been exhibited in various parts of the country. Stanley Franklin frequently works for television.*

'During the period I was working as editorial cartoonist for the Daily Mirror, Johnny Speight's creation emerged. Fleet Street became fascinated. Speight had put his gifts of perspicacity and humour into the most grotesque box imaginable – Alf Garnett. This brilliant mixture of veracity and vulgarity makes one aware that the dividing line between man's genius and idiocy is so thin it is almost invisible. At least, Alf Garnett can't see it. I certainly can't see it.
Is there an optician in the house?'

The Scripts

"I, Lord Hill, do promise Mary, never to allow the pornographic Old Testament to be heard on BBC religous programmes"

The Bird Fancier

Till Death Us Do Part: No. 3 (4th Series)

Recording: 13th August 1972

Transmission: 20th September 1972

The Bird Fancier

SCENE 1　　The Garnett's living-room — early evening. Else is in the armchair, gently rocking Rita's baby. Rita and Mike are reading on the settee.
　　　　　　All is quiet and peaceful. Suddenly the baby wakes up and bawls its head off.

　　　　　　(*Long pause*)

ELSE　　　That'll be your Dad. (*Rises — gives baby to Rita and goes to kitchen*)

　　　　　　(*Baby carries on bawling. Else takes plate of food out of oven and re-enters living room — puts plate on table, takes top plate off — goes back to kitchen — puts plate on gas stove — goes back into living room — sits in chair*)

BABY　　　(*is still bawling*)

ALF　　　　(*enters — takes off coat — sits down to his meal*)

　　　　　　(*Else ignores him*)

25

ALF	(*puts on salt and pepper — picks up knife and fork — stops, puzzled*) How d'you know I was coming in?
ELSE	(*points at baby*) By young Michael — as soon as you turn the corner he starts to cry.

(*Alf glares at her*)

BABY	(*Still bawling*)
ELSE	It's funny that...how that child can sense him...
RITA	Oh Mum, it's just coincidence.
ELSE	Well, it strikes me strange. As soon as he turns by that corner shop..young Michael starts...
ALF	Well, you're wrong, ain't you? 'Cos I didn't come that way tonight.
BABY	(*Bawls even louder*)
ELSE	It doesn't matter what way you come...that child knows.
ALF	Shut up!

(*Baby immediately stops crying. Evevrybody reacts*)

ALF	Yes, he knows...the voice of authority. (*He shovels food into his mouth — it's still hot from the oven. Lets out a yell as he burns himself*) Aahhh...(*Spits food back on to plate*)
ELSE	(*disgusted*) Pig!
ALF	Not my fault. You made me burn myself (*Eats, blowing food first*) Where d'you get this meat?
ELSE	Why? What's wrong with it now?
ALF	Nothing. It's not bad, that's all — for a change.
ELSE	It should be all right — it's best English lamb.
ALF	English? How d'you know it's bloody English?
ELSE	'Cos it said so on the label.
ALF	Label! They can put anything on labels these days. Can't go by bloody labels. I mean, blimey — they could put English labels on Pakistanis, couldn't they? But it wouldn't make 'em bloody English, would it...?
ELSE	That should be English that lamb should. It was thirty pence dearer than New Zealand lamb, it was...
ALF	Well, that's yer bloody Labour Government that is, annit? It was them that gave yer farmers their bloody subsidies, wasn't it? That's what's wrong with our economics — see — yer New Zealand — they grow lambs like we do — they feed 'em like we do — and when they get ready for eating, they kill 'em like we do. And then — yer New Zealand— they freeze their lambs — and then they transport 'em thousands of miles across New Zealand and put 'em on a boat and then transport 'em thousands of miles across the sea to England. And they *still* end up on your table cheaper than yer Canterbury lambs from down the road!

MIKE	(*reacts*) Canterbury is in New Zealand.
ALF	Well, that's where you're wrong — 'cos Canterbury is in Kent — you ignorant scouse git!
MIKE	I'm talking about the Canterbury in New Zealand where the lambs come from ..
ALF	And I'm talking about the Canterbury in Kent where the Archbishop of Canterbury comes from.
ELSE	He comes from Lambeth.
ALF	He comes from Kent.
ELSE	Well, he spends all his time in Lambeth.
ALF	He spends all his time in the Canterbury Cloisters.
ELSE	What's that?
MIKE	It's a pub down the Old Kent Road.
ALF	You heathen scouse git!
MIKE	What's so wrong about old Ramsey having a drink, then?
ELSE	Well, if he does, Michael, he's not setting a very good example to those young lads of his.
RITA	What lads? Old Ramsey hasn't got any children.
ELSE	You know who I'm talking about. Those lads who play for him. You can't expect those lads to go and win matches if he keeps 'em out drinking all night.

RITA   Mum! The Archbishop of Canterbury isn't the England team manager. That's *Alf* Ramsey. (*They laugh*)

ELSE   (*a bit piqued*) He wears Archbishop's gaiters.

MIKE   They're his track suit trousers... (*They laugh again*)

ELSE   Hm... Well, perhaps it's a pity the Archbishop's not their team manager. Because if he was they might behave a bit better. It might stop them swearing an' kicking at each other. Young hooligans.

ALF   Bloody daft as they come she is, ain't she?

RITA   The Archbishop of Canterbury...Manager of England! (*Laughs*)

ELSE   Anyone can make a mistake, Rita.

ALF   It wouldn't be such a bloody bad idea anyway if he was. At least he wouldn't have betrayed us to the Germans like Sir Bloody Alf did.

MIKE   Eh?

ALF   Never bloody mind, eh. He sold us out to the Germans for a handful of Deutschmarks — for a mess of porridge — bloody Judas.

MIKE   Where did you get hold of that idea?

ALF   Bloody fact, annit? It's international scandal...the whole world knows yer Germans couldn't beat England — A Knight of the Realm — an' he does that — they ought to put him in the bloody Tower an' shoot him.

MIKE   You don't half come out with some bloody stories you do.

ALF   Look, it's fact. I got it from a good source.

MIKE   Where?

ALF   Up the pub.

RITA   Up the pub! A right source of information that place is.

ELSE   A hot bed of scandal more like it.

ALF   Blimey...hark who's talking! When you an' old Gran get in there — with yer port an' gins — no one's reputation is safe. The other night in there — old Gran — she was spreading scandal about Heaven she was...saying — she was — that...that Mary couldn't be a virgin — 'cos she was in child by...(*looks reverently upwards*) Him.

ELSE   (*is shocked*)

ALF   I thought she'd get struck down any minute, I did — I walked away. I wasn't the only one either.

ELSE   Well...I suppose they're different to us — up there. I suppose they can have babies without having to do what we have to do.

RITA   (*reacts sympathetically*)

ALF   Yer...I know...well, what they do is immaculate, annit?

MIKE	I wonder how many they've got now?
ELSE	Who?
MIKE	HIM and HER
ELSE	They only had the one.
MIKE	Yeah — but that was two thousand years ago — they could have had another fifteen hundred by now.
ELSE	(*is not amused*)
MIKE	Unless they're on the pill.
ALF	(*explodes*) You. . .!! I only hope He can hear you — you blasphemous scouse git!
MIKE	I wonder if they get any family allowance an' all that?
RITA	The Queen does.
ALF	Yer — so she might — and she'll bloody well need it — if your Labour lot have their way. . .Oooooh . .oh .(*holds his breast*) Ooooh. . .
ELSE	You having another heart attack?
ALF	It wouldn't bother you would it? It wouldn't bother you if I was.
ELSE	Well — you have so many.
ALF	It's a pain (touches his chest) Right here it is. . .in me. . .pimples.
RITA	Might be a sex change. (*giggles*)
ALF	Shurrup.
MIKE	Where d'you fancy going for the operation? (*laughs*)
ALF	Shurrup you. . !
MIKE	Come on — get your coat on and buy us a drink out of your Post War Credits.
ALF	(*tries to shut him up — but he's too late*)
ELSE	Post War Credits? Have you got 'em?
ALF	Yers — an' I'm bloody keeping 'em (touches his breast gingerly) Oooh. . .I felt something dig in me last night (to Else) Probably them iron things you wear in your bloody hair.
ELSE	Well — I try and look nice for you.
ALF	Nice!
RITA	How much did you get Dad?
ALF	(pulling out money) Eighty two pounds.
ELSE	Go on! Is it tax free?

ALF   Course it's tax free — it's a rebate — you silly moo. There ought to be a few thousand pounds interest on it too — the time they've had it — bloody government! They start bloody wars they can't afford — then they have to come on the earhole to us — expect us to pay for 'em. That old fool Chamberlain that was...'Peace in our time'...an' hardly a bleeding month later he's on the wireless — 'No undertaking having been given..'is Majesty's Government has no alternative but to declare war on Germany'...Didn't give a thought to the cost of it — didn't enter his head to go into a few figures — get an estimate — soppy old sod.

ELSE   You were as pleased as punch that Sunday — when they declared war — you was the first one out in the street. Running up the road cheering you was — until the air raid siren went — then you almost broke your neck trying to get down the shelter.

ALF Look, I wasn't against the war. All I'm saying — if they was gonna have it, they ought to have saved up for it. I mean — Churchill told 'em that too, didn't he — it wasn't only me. Even borrowed money off the Yanks they did — but I bet the bloody Americans done better than what I done — I bet they got a bit of bloody interest on what they lent 'em. Anyway if you want me to buy you a drink, you'd better get your coats on, the pair of you. (*counts the money*)

ELSE Half of that money's mine anyway.

ALF Eh?

ELSE 'Cos while you was lending that to old Chamberlain...

ALF Look...

ELSE I had to go short...

ALF Look...

ELSE I had to scrimp an' save...

ALF Listen...

ELSE And try and make do...

ALF Well, so did I!

ELSE I know you did.

ALF I had to go short too...

ELSE I know you did.

ALF Well then...

ELSE So...*half* of it's yours (*takes money from Alf, measures the two piles of money and hands one half to Alf. Keeps the rest herself. Alf is speechless. Else beams at him*)

SCENE 2 Interior pub — later that evening. Gran and Else sit talking. Gran is well stoned.

GRAN (*drinks*) Them single deckers — not real buses. . .

ELSE Everything's changing now Gran — all these new flats. (*Else points through window of pub to high rise flats towering above*)

GRAN Got to pass the conductor now — got to pay him — 'fore you get on. In the old days — on yer real buses — they had upstairs to 'em — didn't they? Eh? Could get on the back way with them an' get upstairs — get down the front — an' make out you was asleep — an' (*winks at Else*) an' no one asked yer for yer fare. . .see? Make yerself comfortable — an' no one bothered yer. Except. . . (*leans nearer to Else*). . .got bothered once though.

ELSE Ooh. .er

GRAN Wasn't the conductor though — wasn't him — sure it wasn't him. But I couldn't open my eyes you see — in case it was him — 'cos I hadn't got the fare y'see. Kept his hand there though. (*Else is suitably shocked*) Kept his hand there from Aldgate to Wapping — didn't take he's hand off till we got to the Causeway. Only took it off then I suppose because he had to get off himself. Unless it *was* the conductor — and I had two more stops to go — so I couldn't open my eyes till then — in case it was. (*chuckles to herself*) Well whoever he was — he was very gentle. Not like some you met in them days — all grab. (*wistfully*) Wish I'd had the fare — seen what he was like.

(*Mike brings drinks over*)

ELSE What about Gran?

MIKE Here y'are — I got her a gin.

ELSE (*to Gran*) D'you want anything in it Gran?

GRAN	Just another gin if you like luv. (*to George — an old Cockney*) What's wrong with your chickens? Ain't they laying?
GEORGE	No — gone right off they have (*points out of the window to top floor of new flats. They all look up*) Being up there I s'pose — seems to have unsettled 'em. Well — they can't get a proper scratch y'see... (*does scratching action with his hand*) I've put earth down — put a sprinkle down like — but they don't seem happy. I mean across the road, before they moved us — I mean we didn't have much garden, but it suited the birds better — they could dig about in it — but up there y'see — it's all that Parquet flooring (*does digging action*) — they can't seem to get their claws going. The worms don't last long up there either. No — it's no place for chickens up there. Well, she's not happy either — the missis. Well, she won't use the lift, frightened of it she is. I missed her for about a week when we first moved in, I found her half way down the stairs. Hearth stoning them she was — silly cow.
ALF	(*Enters from gents*) Hey, Bert — what are you going to do with your pigeons then? Eh? When they move you up into one of them new flats?
BERT	They'll be alright Alf — they ain't like chickens (*look at George*) — they got wings mate... (*flaps his arms*) They can fly.
GEORGE	Chickens 'as got wings.
BERT	Can't fly though.
GEORGE	They can flutter.
BERT	(*to Alf*) I've won medals with them pigeons (*undoes his coat to reveal rows of medals around his belt*). Here are — look — all for speed them nearly — couple there for war service. That one there — that's like yer pigeons Victoria Cross that is. Got that at Dunkirk he did — good bird he was — brave! He had heart bigger'n he'self he had — that one.
ALF	What happened then?
BERT	Rung his neck
ALF	Eh?

BERT — Well, he lost a couple of races and with the price of food you can't afford to keep losers. Didn't like doing it, it was hard to face him, so I shut my eyes. He ate well too, very tasty. Came in handy with the food rations — supplemented the meat rations.

GRAN — ... yer ... I wish I'd had the fare. I could have opened me eyes then, seen what he was like.

(*Alf joins Mike at bar*)

ALF — What's she on about?

MIKE — On about a grope she had in 1914...

BERT — (*crossing to Alf*) I got six birds now that are so fast — I tell you what, I took 'em up to Liverpool the other week, let 'em go, an' they was back here before I was.

ALF — Gerrorfff.

BERT — True.

ALF — What d'yer do ... walk?

BERT — Nope. I come back on the train.

ALF — (*laughs*) What — was there a go-slow on?

MIKE — That train does the bloody ton.

BERT — Ton or no bloody ton mate — my birds beat it.

ALF — Gerrorff — you're bloody mad you are. The bloody pigeon ain't been born yet that can fly hundred miles an hour...

BERT — Mine can.

ALF — Well I'll bet you a bloody pound they can't.

ALF (*getting out his Post War Credits*) Yer ... (*to Bert*) Here —make that another fiver then — all right?

Yer, suits me.

BERT (*They both hand money to barman*)

ALF (*indicating Bert's money*) Hey — they real?

BERT They're as good as yours mate. You ain't the only one who's got Post War Credits...

MIKE (*whispers to Alf*) Make it more ...

ALF Eh?

MIKE You're on a bloody good thing ain't yer?

ALF Yer ... stone bonker annit? (*to Bert*) Here — make it another ten.

BERT Alright.

(*They both give more money to the barman*)

MIKE I'll have five...

ALF Yer — I'll have another five too (*puts down cash*) — here y'are.

MIKE (*taking Alf's money*) My five too. Blimey, he's got no chance, has he? Bloody old fool, him an' he's bloody pigeons, he'll have to pawn their medals after this. (*laughs*)

SCENE 3 **Lime Street Station, Liverpool. Alf and Bert alight from train carrying pigeon basket.**

BERT You ready for the moment of liberation?

ALF The what?

BERT Liberation — the 'off'!

ALF Oh yer... I'm ready.

(*Bert opens the basket and lets his pigeons go. We see them circle round over the station*)

BERT They're off...

ALF (*looking up*) They ain't gone yet.

BERT They're being fair ain't they? They're giving the train a chance to get started. Come on.

BERT Alright.

ALF (*to barman*) Here — put that behind the bar Fred. (*gives him money*)

BARMAN How you gonna prove it?

ALF I'll go up to Liverpool with him — don't worry.

BARMAN It'll cost you more than that in fares..

(*Bert closes his basket and Alf and he climb into London train. As the train moves off the pigeons land on the train roof*)

SCENE 4 Interior Inter-city express train. Buffet bar. Alf and Bert are drinking heavily. Alf looks out of window at motorway. The train is tearing along passing all the cars on the road. Alf is boozily jubilant.

ALF Ha ha ha — look at her go! She's passing everything! Look — look at that Rolls Royce — look — it looks like it's going backwards — ha ha ha. Your bloody pigeons have got no chance.

BERT Make it another ten then.

ALF You sure?

BERT Yer . . . if you want it.

ALF Right you're on — make it twenty if you like.

BERT Done. (*They both count out more money*)

ALF Ha ha ha . . . (*orders more drinks*) See — the trouble with yer Wales and yer

Scotland is, they want to be like us, and have a country of their own, with its own Parliament, and they ain't big enough. I mean, all Wales an' Scotland are really is parts of rural England . . . somewhere to go for your holidays, that's all. What they should be is Counties, like your Devon and Cornwall. I mean, let 'em have their own Lord Mayor, yer. I mean, same with your Ireland, it shouldn't be the Irish Free State, it should be yer *County* of . . .

BERT   Yer, I know that. I mean, I know that. You know that, but they want Home Rule, and their own language.

ALF   What they want is a good thumping. Like we gave 'em in the old days.

BERT   What, have a war with them, you mean?

ALF   No, don't be daft. You can't have a war with them, I mean, all them wars we had with 'em in the old days, they wasn't wars, they was more like blood sports.

BERT   They had their own Queen in them days, didn't they? The Scots did.

ALF   Mary?

BERT   Queen of Scots.

ALF   That cow! She wasn't a proper Queen, tried to get above her station, an' what happened? She got the chop, didn't she? Yer, they knew how to handle 'em in those days. Yer Jocks are all right anyway. They don't cause much bother, 'cept at football. They're not bad at that actually, some of 'em. A bit dirty, but then all their brains is in their feet;

(*Barmen re-enters with more drinks. Alf and Bert knock them back*)

BERT   Here, them Welsh has got their own language, an' they? We had one with us in the Army. Nice bloke, but proper ignorant though. He couldn't speak English hardly at all. All he knew was this sort of Welsh lingo. (*chuckles*) We used to have a laugh at him.

ALF   Yer I know, they're a thick lot.

BERT   He said that everyone in he's village spoke this sort of Welsh language.

ALF   It's not a language really, it's a kind of dialect.

BERT   No, he had his own words an' everything. He had words for drink, an' for eating.

ALF   Well, your natives have that. They have *sounds* for things, but it's not language. I mean, a dog barks but it's not language. I mean, yer Jocks an' yer Irish they've got that, they've got sounds. Yer Gaelic. . .but it's no good to 'em 'cept for talking among themselves. They wanna talk to other people, they've got to learn English. Trouble is — it's beyond their grasp, for most of 'em, I mean yer Welsh. I mean, we even had to teach them how to dig coal! See — the trouble with your average Taffy, see he's nothing much more than a two-legged pit pony really In fact, yer pit pony could pull more coal, *and* was cheaper to run. Blimey, I tell you what, if yer mine owners had their way, yer Welsh would be extinct by now. Blimey, they was getting rid of them faster than your Julius Caesar and he's Romans did . . . You know, it's a pity they ain't got no coal mines out in Ireland, 'cos they're good with shovels, yer Micks are.

BERT   Yer, it's what you're born to, I suppose.

ALF   That's it. I mean, give a Mick a shovel an' a big hole an' he'll keep digging till he comes up the other end.

(*An American tourist enters buffet*)

YANK   Can I have two bourbons on the rocks?

BERT   Hang on, we've got one here.

ALF   What?

BERT   A Taffy

BARMAN   Got no bourbon, mate.

YANK   Any rye?

ALF   He ain't Welsh.

BERT   He ain't English.

ALF   You can always tell your Welsh 'cos they speak like Pakistanis. You can also tell your Welsh by their faces, they've all got holes in their faces.

BERT   Trying to use a knife and fork?

ALF   No, it's coal pox. They used to carry all the dust home in their faces, an' the mines were losing thousands until they installed showers and made 'em wash 'fore they went home. (*to American*) Afternoon.

YANK   (*nods*) Hi there.

ALF   (*to Bert*) American — he's American. (*to American*) Over here visiting the old country?

BERT   Old country?

ALF   Yer, well they was part of us in the old days, wasn't yer? You Americans. Speak the same as us, don't yer. Part of the Empire wasn't yer. Part of the old Empire, they was, under us in the old days . . . but you wanted to be independent, wanted to start up on your own, so you come to England like a son might go to he's father, an' said — I'm grown up now and I'd like to go out on my own (*the booze brings tears to his eyes*) and England in her infinite wisdom said, So be it, Yes, you may . . . and you've done well. Been a credit — you've done better than any of the other Colonies. Done better than Australia, and Canada.

BERT   And India

ALF   And Ind. . . *every*body's done better than India. No. No. Credit where it's due, you've done well. (*to Bert*) Done well they have. Admitted we helped 'em, sent some of our best people out there we did, to help 'em get started. (*the American turns away*) No listen. It's true, annit? It's true, and another thing in the early days — when they was struggling out there, when they was short of labour, who was it flogged them all their coons, eh? *Us*. They was our coons. They come out of our Africa, they did. I mean, that's facts that is. We had a surplus of coons sitting about in our Africa doing nothing.

BERT   They weren't sitting around doing nothing, Alf.

ALF   All right, swinging in the bleedin' trees then. (*to the American*) So we exported 'em — exported 'em to your America. 'Course, not saying we didn't do well out of it, but you was grateful for them coons then, wasn't you? I know you ain't too pleased about 'em now, but you was grateful at the time. I bet if the truth is known you wouldn't mind shipping 'em all back again now, would you? (*Bert slips drunkenly from counter — Alf helps him up — both laughing*) Eh? — ha ha ha! Well — we don't want 'em, we've got enough of our own. They . . . they invented that pill too late you know. If you'd have had that in the old days you could have fed your coons on it — we ought to feed 'em on it now. Ram it down their bleedin' throats — or bung 'em all out to Ireland — that'd shut the Micks up. That'd give 'em something to think about wouldn't it . . . Here, do you want to have a bet on his pigeons?

YANK   (*Wishes he'd stayed at home*)

SCENE 5   Euston Station, London. The train arrives and Alf and Bert get out and walk along the platform carrying the basket — or rather stagger along — Alf has a pocket full of miniatures. They stop while Alf gets a couple out — and hands one to Bert.

ALF   (*drinking*) To our four feathered . . . friends . . . *my* four feathered friends (*hiccups*) Right?

BERT   My . . . four feathered friends Alf . . .

ALF   (*shaking his head drunkenly*) Nope . . . mine . . .

(They stagger from station — and hail taxi. They climb in as taxi drives off the pigeons land on its roof)

SCENE 6	Bert's back yard. Everyone from the pub is there. Pigeon loft in background. Barman is serving drinks from a barrel of beer in foreground. Alf and Bert enter. Alf is still laughing.
ALF	Ha ha. . .! Ha ha. . .! Well — here we are. . .!
MIKE	So are the pigeons.
	(Alf stares. We hear the pigeons cooing)
ELSE	They arrived three minutes before you did.
ALF	*(speechless)* Eh?
	(Bert roars with laughter — collects his winnings from the pub barman)
ALF	*(reacts)* I'm going up the pub!
BARMAN	We're closed!
	(Everyone roars with laughter. A pigeon drops it load on Alf's bald head)

I can give it up any time I like...

Till Death Us Do Part: No. 4 (2nd Series)

Recording: 22nd December 1966

Transmission: 16th January 1967

I can give it up any time I like...

SCENE 1   The Garnetts' living room. The family are sitting watching television. Mike is coughing loudly and persistently. Alf glares at him, annoyed.

ALF   Shut that noise up! Blimey, how can you listen to the telly with all that coughing in your earhole.

RITA   Look, it's not Mike's fault he's got a cold, Dad. Blimey, he's not doing it on purpose.

ELSE   (*smoking*) It's all that smoking — that's what makes him cough.

ALF   Blimey, the bloody telly's bad enough as it is, without him coughing all through it. Terrible it is on there some nights. Bloody awful. (*Lights his pipe and starts to fill the room with smoke, making Mike cough more*) Got worse, too, I think, since Labour's been in power.

MIKE   (*coughing*) Don't be...don't be daft. What's it...what's it got to do with Labour? Labour don't pick the programmes.

ALF   Look, it's your Postmaster General what's in charge of it, annit? An' he's Labour.

MIKE   The ITA has got nothing to do with the Postmaster General.

ALF   Well, I ain't saying it has, am I?

MIKE   But it's ITA you're watching, annit? Not BBC.

ALF   I know, because I had to turn the BBC's load of rubbish off, didn't I? I'll turn this lot off as well. (*Turns TV off. Fills his pipe and lights it again*) Another thing — yer Lord Hill...

MIKE   Eh?

RITA   What Lord Hill?

ALF   You know who I'm talking about — Lord Hill — the one what runs your ITA — him.

MIKE   Well, what about him?

ALF   Who does he have to make his report to, eh?

ELSE   Wasn't he the Radio Doctor? Oh, I liked him.

ALF   The Government, you hairy Nellie, that's who...

ELSE   He cured my lumbago once, he did.

ALF   Look....

ELSE   I wrote to him...

ALF   Look...

ELSE   An' told him how I had this lumbago.

ALF   Look...

ELSE   An' he wrote back.

ALF   Look...

ELSE   Very nice letter he wrote.

ALF   Look...

ELSE   Told me what to do with it, he did.

ALF   Look...

ELSE   I think we was all a lot healthier when he was on the radio.

ALF   Look!

ELSE   What?

ALF   I lost me thread now, you great pudden!

MIKE   He ought to have stayed on the radio — we might be getting some better television programmes if he had.

ALF   Look, you can't blame Lord Hill. Because he's a Tory by his convictions, but he's under the subserviance of your Labour Government. 'Cos they got their dirty hands in everything, ain't they?

ELSE   They never have him in that Emergency Ward Ten, do they?

RITA   Who?

ELSE   The Radio Doctor.

RITA   Oh, don't be daft, Mum.

ELSE   Well, he'd be better than some they have on it. I mean, if he's in charge of it, he ought to be able to get himself in some of the programmes. He was good on the radio, he was. Very good.

RITA   He's a politician now, Mum.

ELSE   Well, so is your Harold Wilson, but he appears on the telly enough.

ALF   Too much if you ask me. (*Fills his pipe and lights it. Starts to fill the room with smoke again. Mike lights a fag and starts to cough like mad*)

RITA   If you had any sense you'd give up smoking till you got over that cold.

MIKE   (*coughing*) What's the point — with him filling the room with that poisonous stuff of his.

ALF   Your pipe tobacco though is healthier than your fag tobacco, annit?

RITA   None of it's any good.

ALF   But your facts prove it, dun they? Your statistics state categorically that it's healthier to smoke a pipe than smoke fags. I mean, all your top politicians — your people in the know — the ones that have seen the figures — I mean, they're all on pipes and cigars, an they? Even that bloody fool Wilson. I mean, he smokes a pipe, dun he? You smoke one of these you'll come to no harm.

MIKE   (*coughs*) No . . . all you do is poison everyone else.

RITA — Look, why don't you stop smoking, Mike — give it up. Just till you get over your cold at least.

MIKE — (*coughing*) Yer, I think I will.

ALF — (*chuckles*) He couldn't give it up. Need will power to do that, an' he ain't got it — that's the trouble.

MIKE — I could give it up.

ALF — *You*? You're too self-indulgent. That's the trouble with your youth today — self-indulgence.

MIKE — Alright, alright, I'll tell you what I'll do — *I'll* give it up if *you* do.

ALF — But I don't need to give it up, do I?

MIKE — Just to prove you can, come on. . .

ALF — (*grins disparagingly*) Look, if I wanted to. . .

MIKE — Come on. . .look, talk's easy — give it up.

ALF — But I don't need to, do I?

MIKE — Never mind about all that, I'm throwing a challenge out — I'll give it up as long as you can. Come on, we'll soon see who's got the will power.

ALF — Look. . .

RITA — He knows he can't, that's why.

ALF — Look. . .look, I can give it up as long as he can, don't worry about that.

MIKE — Alright — are you on then?
(*Alf sits silently for a while, struggling with himself*).

MIKE — See, he can't — he's all mouth and trousers.

RITA — 'Course he is.

ALF — (*annoyed*) Alright. Alright. You're on. You're on. (*Still smoking*)

ELSE — Well, put that out then.

ALF — Look — let him put his out first.

MIKE — Alright — here we go. (*Stubs out fag*) That's me last fag.

ALF — (*reluctantly knocks his pipe out*) Yer? You'll weaken 'fore I do. . .you see. . .

MIKE — Yer, we'll see. Oh, and to make it fair we'll have two referees — Mum and Rita. We'll put all the money we normally spend on fags and tobacco in a box, and whichever one of the two catches either of us smoking, gets the kitty. That should make them very good spies. Fair?

ELSE — Sounds fair to me.

ALF — Alright, you scouse git, alright.

MIKE — Right. Now we'll see who's got all the will power.

ALF — Yers. We will. We will. Yers. (*Sits glowering in filthy temper, and then starts to suck stem of his empty pipe*)

MIKE	Hey, hey, hey! Look! (*Points*)
ALF	I ain't smoking. That pipe's empty.
MIKE	But you're getting comfort from it and that's not fair. Hand it over. Come on.
ALF	Look, that's my pipe — that's my pipe!
MIKE	(*picks up cigarettes*) Look, I'll chuck these on the fire, you chuck yours on.
ALF	Eh? I ain't chucking. . .
MIKE	Now who's got will power, eh? Come on, come on, both together. (*Throws packet of cigarettes on fire*) There goes mine — now you. Come on. (*Throws Alf's tobacco on fire*) And the pipe — come on.

(*Mike throws Alf's pipe on fire and jams it down with poker. Alf picks up fag packet from fire*)

ALF	You scouse git! Look! One fag you've thrown on there. I've sacrificed an ounce of tobacco and me genuine briar, straight grain.
MIKE	Well, you won't need 'em will you, 'cos you're not going to smoke any more, are you?
ALF	Alright, alright. We'll see. I didn't serve in the desert for nothing. Living on iron tack. (*Else yawns*) I tell you, you'll crack first. An' I'll let you sweat, you long-haired git. 'Cos I won't give in — never!
ELSE	Huh!

(*Alf sits glowering for a while. Then he jumps up*)

ALF	I'm going to bed. (*Exits*)
RITA	You've done it now. He'll be impossible to live with now.
ELSE	He's been impossible to live with for the last thirty years.

SCENE 2   The living room: next evening. The family are sitting watching television. Alf sits between Rita and Else who are smoking. As Else draws on her cigarette, she is watched by Alf, hungrily. He almost inhales with her. Else blows smoke out, then Rita draws on her cigarette — again watched by Alf. Repeat this business several times to show Alf's craving for a smoke. He turns from one to the other as they smoke. Mike ignores it and watches telly. Alf looks at Mike. . .fidgets. . .and watches the women smoking once more. Finally Alf turns to Mike.

ALF How are you getting on with not smoking, then?

MIKE Don't miss 'em at all.

(*Alf reacts with a glare, and watches the women smoking again*)

MIKE How are *you* getting on?

ALF Oh — the same. Same. (*Pause as he watches the two women smoking*) Only I was thinking. . .I mean, if you're finding it a bit of a strain like. . .well, I mean, you wanna turn the bet in. . .I don't mind, like. I mean, you've proved yourself. You've proved you've got the will power. I mean, there'd be no shame in it. . .I mean, if you wanna turn it in, like. . .

MIKE No, I'm fine. I don't want to start smoking any more. I feel much better without fags. Me cough's gone. I'm eating better — I can taste things now. I feel marvellous, don't you?

ALF (*glowering*) Oh — yer. . .yer. . .bloody marvellous. (*Glares at TV*)

(*BBC News comes on TV*)

NEWSCASTER Mr. Wilson arrived at London Airport this afternoon where he was met by Mr. George Brown. . . (*etc.*)

ALF Look at him! Bloody fool Wilson — what does he look like, eh? What *does* he look like? Blimey, it's about time he bought himself a new raincoat, annit? The money he's earning. . .he goes out an' meets dignitaries wearing that old thing. . .I wonder what they must think? Look at him now! He ain't hardly off the plane an' he's got his pipe going already!

RITA   What's wrong with that?

ALF   What's wrong? Disgusting, annit? That's what's wrong. . .smoking his pipe on telly like that, in full view of the Nation.

RITA   Disgusting? What's wrong with smoking a pipe? You smoke one.

ALF   Well, that's where you're wrong, Miss Smartypants, annit? 'Cos I don't, do I? 'Cos I've give it up, an I? Same as he ought to. I mean, if smoking's so bad, he ought to set an example to the Nation, didn't he? An' give it up hisself.

MIKE   Look, he don't smoke on television when he appears as Prime Minister.

ALF   What's he appearing as now then, eh? I mean, he's on there, now, smoking — an he?

MIKE   Look, he's just got off an airplane, an he? Blimey, I mean, he's off duty. The man's just having a smoke, that's all!

ALF   Look, mate, never mind about just having a smoke. You've never seen Her Majesty with a fag stuck in Her mouth. Whether She's appearing on television, catching a train up Sandringham, or anywhere She appears. You've never seen that woman with a fag on.

ELSE   Nor *Him*. You never see *Him* with a fag in his mouth neither.

ALF   I mean, what she does in her own house is her own affair. But you never see her smoking in public.

ELSE   Nor *Him*. You never see *Him*, neither.

ALF   'Cos they've been brought up with a bit of discipline, *they* have. I mean, all your Monarchs, they're in the Army or the Navy at no age, doing a bit of service, getting their knees browned a bit.

ELSE   The Queen wasn't in the Navy.

ALF   *He* was. . .

ELSE   She wasn't in the Army, either. She was in the A.T.S.

ALF   The A.T.S. is the female department of the Army, annit, you silly great pudden! An' your Royals, when they're born as children, they're born to rule, an' they're brought up to it. Not like your politicians. I mean, half of them are dragged up, especially your Labour lot. Come out of slums they do, most of them. That is why Her Majesty should have a veto, and be allowed to over-rule the Parliament any time she wants to.

RITA   Rubbish.

ALF   Not rubbish. That is yer democracy, annit?

MIKE   What are you talking about — 'democracy'? Blimey — that's the opposite to democracy, that is. Democracy is *all* having a vote, annit? *All* having a say about who runs the country — that's democracy.

ALF   Well, that's where you're wrong, annit, you scouse git.

RITA   He's not wrong.

ALF   Listen a minute — listen. . . They had a National Opinion Poll a little while ago didn't they, eh? A National Opinion Poll about whether the Queen should be able to over-rule yer Parliament. And sixty per cent of the country — sixty per cent — said yes, she ought to. And if they don't let her, then that's not democracy is it? 'Cos sixty per cent is a majority. . .an' the majority want her to be able to over-rule Wilson and run the country herself.

MIKE   Oh, don't talk rubbish.

ALF   That's not rubbish, mate, that's facts, that is. Look, if Her Majesty stood for Parliament — if the Tory Party had any sense and made Her its leader instead of that grammar school twit Heath — us Tories, mate, would win every election we went in for.

ELSE   She wouldn't want to go to all them political meetings. . .

ALF   Look. . .

ELSE   With people throwing stink bombs. . .and the language. . .

ALF   Look!

ELSE   No, I don't think that sort of thing would appeal to Her. Not the way She's been brought up.

ALF   But *He* could. *He* could stand. *He* wouldn't be embarrassed by anything like that. I mean — Philip — he's been in the Navy, an he? So I mean, he's heard a bit of bad language before. Make a good Prime Minister too, he would.

MIKE   Make a good polo player.

ALF   Look, he'd make a bloody sight better Prime Minister than your Harold Wilson, anyway.

MIKE Gerroff! Philip as Prime Minister — blimey, he's got no knowledge of Parliamentary procedure for a start. I mean, if he stood up in the House of Commons, they'd tear him to pieces they would.

ALF Don't you be so sure.

MIKE Michael Foot would.

RITA So would Mikardo.

MIKE And Zilliacus.

ALF Bloody foreigners, shouldn't be in the Parliament for a start — bloody Greeks.

MIKE So is Philip — he's a Greek too.

ALF But he's a different sort of Greek. He's not one of your restaurant Greeks, he's a *Royal* Greek. A gentleman.

(*Mike and Rita hoot with laughter*)

ALF (*furious*) I'm going to bed!

ELSE Yer — well, before you go to bed (*shakes tin at him*) don't forget your day's 'no tobacco money'.

ALF You *would* have to remind me about not smoking. (*He and Mike put money in tin*)

SCENE 3 The living room. Else is smoking and ironing some hankies, watched by Alf, who is hypnotised by her smoking. Else puts her fag in ashtray and turns away from it and Alf in order to put the ironing on sideboard and pick up another garment to iron.

Alf puts his hand out stealthily for fag. He has his hand almost on it when Else turns back. He pulls his hand away just in time. Else has another draw on cigarette and then puts it in ashtray. She turns away again.

Alf leans towards ashtray and almost gets his lips to cigarette when Else turns back. He pulls away from it again. This business is repeated several times.

Else turns back once more to cigarette — and stubs it out under Alf's hungry gaze. She turns away again. Alf looks at her packet of cigarettes on the table. He puts his hand out towards them — she turns — he whips his hand away. When she turns away again, he picks up newspaper and places it over the cigarettes — then he picks up the paper with the cigarettes in it — holds paper up in front of his face — takes one cigarette out of packet — then puts paper back on table with cigarettes underneath.

Alf rises nonchalantly and leaves the room. He goes outside to the toilet. He enters toilet, sits on seat, puts fag in his mouth. As he strikes match —

MIKE (*off*) What are you doing in there?

ALF (*jumps guiltily, puts fag in pocket, blows match out*) What d'you think I'm doing in here, you nosey scouse git!

(He sits glaring for a few seconds, then craftily puts his eye to a knothole in the door. He is confronted by another eye, obviously Mike's. Alf jumps away quickly — stands up — tears paper off toilet roll, rustles it loudly, puts it in toilet — pulls chain — and leaves toilet.

Mike is in the living-room when Alf enters it. He sits down, glaring. After a few seconds he yawns)

ALF I think I'll go up to bed. Got a hard day tomorrow. (*Exits*)

SCENE 4 Alf's bedroom. Alf enters, grinning to himself. He goes to the window, opens it, puts fag in mouth, strikes match — and hears Mike's voice again.

MIKE You feel like a bit of fresh air as well, do you?

(Alf hastily puts match out and looks out of window. He sees Mike in street below and slams window angrily. Alf stands in the middle of the bedroom, fuming. His eyes wander to fireplace. He starts to grin again.

He goes over to fireplace, looks up chimney, mimes blowing smoke up – grins. He takes out last match and lights it, but the draught from the chimney blows it out. He is livid – kneels on floor, fuming.

The bedroom door opens and Else enters. Alf quickly places cigarette between his hands and joins them, ostensibly in prayer. Else looks at him and starts to get undressed)

SCENE 5   The same bedroom: a couple of hours later. Else is gently snoring. Alf opens his eyes and looks at her. He smiles, and taking his cigarette from under the pillow, tiptoes round the bed. He pauses by bedside table on her side, takes her matches, and creeps out of room.

At Mike and Rita's door he stops and listens to them snoring too, then he smiles and creeps quietly downstairs.

He enters toilet – smiles – puts cigarette in his mouth – takes out a match and strikes it. It won't light. Alf frowns and looks at it, and realises that it's a spent match. He throws it down and takes out another match – looks at it and scowls again. He throws it down and takes out another match. This too is a spent one. He pulls a few more out, all spent. He pulls out more – all spent. He explodes in rage.

ALF   Silly bloody moo! (*As he says this the fag falls from his mouth and drops into toilet*) Now look what she's made me do! Putting used matches back in the box!

SCENE 6 The living-room: the following evening. Alf is sitting puffing away at his pipe with obvious enjoyment. Mike and Rita enter — they do a double take at Alf smoking.

MIKE Hello! What's all this? (*Alf smiles up at Mike*) So I win, eh? You cracked up, didn't you? So who's got the will power, then, eh? 'When I was in the desert . . .'! Who cracked? *You* did, didn't you, eh? Who's got the will power, eh?

ALF Will power — well, I mean, you might have the will power to *stop* smoking, but what I've got — what *I've* got — is the will power to *start* smoking again, and to keep on smoking.

MIKE Eh? What are you talking about? What kind of will power is that?

ALF Never mind about that, mate. I'm smoking for the health and prosperity of the country. . .

RITA For what?

ALF Where does the Nation derive its biggest income from, eh? Yer tobacco tax, annit? So, I mean, if the whole country stopped smoking, all that money's down the drain, annit? Almost come under your Sabotage Act, wouldn't it? Ruining the country's economy. No, you see — I mean, it's patriotic to smoke, annit? Another thing, d'you know that the amount of money collected on tobacco tax last year was enough to pay for the entire National Health Service, an' a bit over. . . I mean (*puffing away*) blimey, us smokers ought to get a medal for what we're doing for the country. I mean, people like you, mate, who are frightened to smoke because of health reasons — I mean, you ought to be given white feathers. . .

MIKE Eh?

ALF Yer. Never mind about 'eh?'. I mean, if a war breaks out — if we declare war on someone, an' you're called to the colours — I mean, you can't refuse to go out an' fight because it's dangerous, can you? Eh? Well, it's the same with yer smoking. . .you don't give that up because it's dangerous, do you? Not if it's for the benefit of your country. No — I'm smoking for England and the Queen!

RITA Well, I caught you — where's the money?

ELSE (*who has been getting ready to go out during all this*) You ready?

ALF Yer, sure. (*Puts his coat and hat on*)

MIKE Where're you going?

ALF Your mother's taking me up the pictures with her winnings, ain't she? I mean, it was her what caught me smoking. . .

ELSE Yer.

ALF So she got all that money out of the tin. After you, my dear — goodnight!

(*They exit — Alf smiling hugely*)

Sex before Marriage

Till Death Us Do Part: No. 2 (2nd Series)

Recording: 8th December 1966

Transmission: 2nd January 1967

Sex before Marriage

SCENE 1   The Garnetts' living room. Alf is standing on a chair trying to hang wallpaper. Mike and Rita are at the table, pasting paper. Rita lets roll of paper go — it shoots up to Mike's end of the table. Rita goes to Mike — they start necking.

ALF   (*seeing them at it*) Leave her alone! (*He tries to slide paper on the wall. It splits. Mike and Rita laugh*) Shut up! How can I concentrate? Bloody paper. Rubbish, it is. It won't hang properly.

RITA   That's not the paper's fault, Dad.

ALF   Not the paper? 'Course it's the bloody paper. Shouldn't have let her pick it, silly moo. If I'd have got it, I'd have got something a bit better than this. Something a bit decent. (*Tries to slide paper — it tears again. Mike and Rita are necking again*)

	Look, gor blimey, stop mucking about with her an' give us another bit of paper up! Blimey, no wonder it won't stick on proper. The bloody paste is dry by the time you hand it up to me.
MIKE	(*hands up paper to him*) Oh, stop moaning. You don't half go on, you do.
ALF	Go on? Blimey, make a bloody saint go on, you lot would.
RITA	Look, if you didn't want to do it, you shouldn't have started it. Mike would have done it.
ALF	*Him*? Shirley Temple? He couldn't stick a fly paper up. It'd be a fat lot of good letting him do anything. (*Brushes paper into place — brush tears a large hole*) Cor, Christ, it's torn again, look! Bloody rubbish. Fancy buying stuff like this. It's as thin as fag paper.
RITA	Oh shut up, Dad. Look, go out. Go to football. We'll do it.
ALF	The bloody walls ain't true, are they?
	(*Else enters carrying tray with cups of tea on it*)
ELSE	Is he still moaning?
RITA	Yes. He hasn't stopped since he started.
ALF	(*trying to repair paper*) Well, I mean. . .you gonna do a job, you ought to have some decent materials to work with. I mean this bloody paper's rubbish.
ELSE	All bad workmen blame their tools.
ALF	Look, you don't shut up I'll walk out an' leave it.
ELSE	I wish you would.
ALF	They ain't even trimmed it proper at the shop.
MIKE	(*holding up paper he has pasted*) D'you want this piece yet?
ALF	Look, give us a chance, I ain't finished this bit yet. . .I can't put two bits up at once, can I?
ELSE	You can't even put one bit up at once.
ALF	(*as he wrecks the paper again*) Oh, gor blimey! Now look what you made me do. Look (*to Mike*) give us another bit of paper. (*Mike hands it to him*) I missed going to football doing this. Gawd! It's all stuck together now.
MIKE	Well, get your finger out. It's been pasted for hours, it's bound to stick, annit?
ALF	Look, don't you start. (*Throws paper down in disgust*) Look, paste up another bit. An' try an' work with me at *my* speed. I mean, any bloody fool can paste up like that, just willy nilly. . .I mean, all you're doing is wasting it, lad.
MIKE	You're the one that's bloody wasting it. You've got more on the floor there than you've got on the wall.
ALF	(*pasting*) Look, that's your fault, annit? If you pasted it proper. . .

MIKE   You keep tearing it. . .

ALF   'Cos you made them all soggy, that's why.

RITA   We ought to have got somebody in — somebody who knows about paper hanging.

ELSE   Yeah.

ALF   (*turns to her*) Look, Miss Bloody Knowall — (*Paper falls off wall behind him. He turns back to wall and sees paper*) *Now* look what you done! (*Picks up paper and sticks it on wall again*) If you'd got a decent pattern instead of bloody flowers. . . How can I work with flowers? They got to be matched up, ain't they? More waste in flowers, too, takes yards more, it does.

ELSE   I liked that pattern, it's cheerful.

ALF   Cheerful! It'll be like sitting in the bloody Botanical Gardens when it's finished.

(*Paper falls down again*)

ELSE   (*picks up paper*) *When* it's finished.

ALF   (*turns to Mike who is standing watching him, brush in hand*) Ain't you pasted that bit up yet?

MIKE   You said to wait for you.

ALF   I didn't say 'wait for me'. I said 'work at my speed'. Now I got to wait for you. Blimey, we'll be on this all night the way you're going.

ELSE   If you hadn't gone down the pub lunchtime, you could have started earlier, couldn't you?

ALF   (*sits*) Eh? What you on about now? I only had a couple, didn't I? It was that Charlie Treacy. . .just had a grandson he has. . .I mean, you got to wet the baby's head, ain't yer?

ELSE   Hm. . .that'll be the day when you need an excuse for drinking.

RITA   I didn't even know Charlie Treacy's daughter was married.

ALF   Well she ain't, is she? But I mean, that don't seem to matter these days, do it? I mean, your church has even brought out a book on it now — *Sex before Marriage*. . . .

(*Else is shocked*)

. . . . The whole country seems to have gone sex mad. I mean. . .had two Bishops on the telly, bold as brass, *talking* about it. Bishops! I mean, when we was young, you never heard people going around talking about sex like that. . .not in public anyway.

ELSE   It used to go on, though.

ALF   I know that. It went on, I know.

ELSE   Yer, well, the other night on the telly. . .I didn't know where to put my face.

Well, I didn't even know the clergy *knew* about them sort of things.

ALF Well, things they were saying. . .I looked at you, didn't I?

ELSE I turned away.

MIKE What were they talking about then?

ALF Eh? What? Blimey, what *wasn't* they talking about. . .

MIKE Look, it's nineteen sixty-seven — you've got to talk about them sort of things.

ALF Not in full view of everyone though. I mean, you go talking about things like that on the telly an' you're going to encourage it, ain't yer?

ELSE Some of 'em don't need much encouraging, if you ask me.

ALF I mean, that sort of thing. . .I mean, it can act like an aphrodaisyac, that sort of thing.

MIKE What sort of thing?

ALF That book yer church has brought out — *Sex before Marriage*.

RITA Oh, you're old fashioned, Dad.

ALF Old fashioned! Look, we was decent-brought up we was, me an' your mother. We didn't. . .I never. . .she and I. . .I didn't have no. . .I didn't attempt to touch your mother till after we was married.

ELSE *Well* after.

ALF (*reacts*) But I didn't touch you before, did I?

ELSE I wouldn't have let you, don't worry.

ALF I didn't *try* though, did I? That's what I'm saying

ELSE No. . .you knew what you'd have got if you had.

RITA   Look, we had no sex either, until we got married. (*Rita catches Mike's expression*) Well, not with me you didn't, anyway.

MIKE   I ain't said nothing, have I?

RITA   But what people do is their own affair and nothing to do with anyone else.

ALF   Before you got married what you did was *my* affair too.

RITA   Well, we didn't do nothing, did we?

MIKE   Blimey, a fat chance we'd have got as well, with him. I only had to come in here for a cup of tea late at night, and he's down them stairs an' sitting here in his long johns till I'd gone.

ALF   Yer – yer – because I didn't trust you, you randy scouse git!

RITA You didn't trust me either.

ALF I trusted you. I've always trusted you. I knew you wouldn't do nothing wrong. It was *him*. He's the one I didn't trust.

MIKE (*rising*) Well, it takes two, dunnit?

ALF You — (*rising, clenching his fists*) you dirty-minded — Are you trying to say my little Rita. . .

MIKE Well, you seem to be saying she would.

ALF I said what? You liar! You bloody liar! I've never said a word against my little girl. . .as He is my Maker, I ain't. . .

ELSE Well, if you did, Michael, it wasn't very nice of you. . .that's all I've got to say.

(*Mike reacts and crosses to Rita*)

ALF If I found out he'd touched my little girl. . .I'd. . .I'd. . .

RITA Oh shut up, for Pete's sake. Look, if we had wanted to do anything like that we could have done it well away from this house, and you would have been none the wiser. And if we had it would have been *our* business an' not *yours*. . .'cos it's *our* lives and not *yours*!

ELSE Oh! I see. (*Rises*) We're beginning to find out things now, are we?

ALF Look. . .did you? Eh? *Did* you?

RITA Mind your own business.

ALF   Look, I'm asking you a question!

RITA   And I'm not going to tell you.

ALF   Look — I'm your father!

RITA   (*kisses his bald head*) Oh stop it, Dad.

ALF   D'you understand?

(*Rita scoots behind Mike*)

ALF   (*to Mike*) Did you? Eh? *Did* you?

MIKE   Eh? Well, I mean, it don't matter what I say, do it? I mean, I'm condemned before I open my mouth, an I?

ELSE   I'm disappointed, Rita. I thought we'd brought you up a bit different to that. I wouldn't have thought you'd let us down like that.

ALF   It's not *her*, it's *him*! Randy Socialist git. They're all the same, they are. Yer Labourites — it's them what started all this free love talk. . .everyone was respectable till they started going around saying it wasn't wrong. They're all the same, yer Socialists — they all want something for nothing — even their love.

(*While he is talking, Mike has pasted up another piece of paper which he holds up to Alf*)

MIKE   Here y'are.

ALF   Stuff it!! (*snatches it and screws it up and hurls it to the floor*)

MIKE   (*looking at it*) Not much use pasting up any more if you're going to do that with it, is there?

ALF   Don't you talk to me. You let him in your house, take him on trust, you do. Let him break bread with you. Let him take your little girl out. Don't ask no questions, you don't. . .and that's how he repays you! That's what he does to her.

MIKE   Cor blimey — annit marvellous?

ELSE   Ain't you got no shame, the pair of you?

RITA   We didn't do nothing, Mum.

ELSE   So *you* say.

RITA   Look, we didn't! We didn't! We didn't!

ELSE   All right, no need to shout. We'll take your word if you say so. No use crying over spilt milk, anyway.

RITA   Oh Gordon Bennett! Look — what have we got to do to make you believe us?

MIKE   I mean, blimey, we didn't get the opportunity for one thing, even if we'd wanted to. . .and there's nowhere you can go round here for a bit of courting. You've got no front porch out there. . .an' if you had, it'd have been a bit embarrassing with him peering through the letter box at us.

ALF Look, shurrup you great nit.

(*Mike and Rita start to paste some more paper*)

RITA Anyway, it's nice to know you trusted us.

(*Pause*)

ALF Look, I didn't say I *didn't* trust you...

ELSE No, your dad didn't say that...

RITA Well Mike didn't do anything, either.

ALF I mean, I didn't think you would do anything like that.

RITA We didn't.

ELSE Not surprised — the way you've been brought up.

RITA We didn't.

ALF It'd have been a surprise to me if you had...

ELSE An' me...

(*Mike and Rita are taken aback at this about turn*)

ALF A big surprise...I mean, you ain't like that Charlie Treacy's girl.

ELSE No.

ALF I know that...

ELSE Me too...

ALF I mean, I've always been able to hold up my head with you, I have...

ELSE Yer. Never heard no whispers about you, we ain't.

RITA Thank you.

MIKE You can hold your head up with the pair of us, Dad.

ALF Yer, well, never mind, son. One day *you'll* be a father. They're good kids really. Look, you don't mind me saying it, son, but look at that paste you've made, it's too thin. It's the wrong consistency, annit? You young people today, you can't keep your mind on the job. I suppose it's us older generation's fault — we've spoilt you. Still, you're only young once... (*Exits to kitchen*)

(*Else, who has been collecting cups, exits with him and shuts door As soon as they've gone Mike and Rita look at each other*)

RITA (*collapses in relief*) Crikey, if they only knew!

MIKE Blimey, the old feller would do his nut! (*They laugh at the thought of it*)

SCENE 2   The kitchen. Alf is at the sink mixing paste and Else is washing cups. There is a long long pause.

ALF   What?

ELSE   Sex before marriage.

ALF   Who did?

ELSE   You. You did. Over at Wanstead it was. In the Green Man. You bought me all them egg flips — tried to get me sozzled, you did.

ALF   Who?

ELSE   You. You did. An' then you tried to get me to go into the Forest with you. (*Laughs*) All that money you spent — an' got nothing. (*Laughs again*)

ALF   Look. . .I wasn't after nothing — it was a short cut through the Forest, that's all.

ELSE   Short cut!!

ALF   It was, I tell you!

ELSE   That's what you say. I knew what you was after. I wasn't daft. Dirty old devil.

ALF   Shut up! You great pudden!

SCENE 3   The living-room. Mike and Rita are still laughing. Wally, the milkman enters.

WALLY   Hello, what's the joke?

RITA   It's the old man — he's been talking about sex.

WALLY   Oh, you shouldn't laugh. When you get to his age that's all you can do — talk about it.

(*Mike and Rita laugh. Alf enters*)

WALLY   Hello, Grandad — you're looking well, considering.

(*Alf glares at him. Else tries to enter over wall-papering mess*)

WALLY   Hello, Cinderella. Don't show us all your laundry — I'm only human.

ELSE   (*giggles*) Saucy devil!

(*Alf glowers*)

WALLY   Here you are — three pints. Anything else?

ELSE   No, that's alright.

WALLY   Don't you want some yoghurt for the old 'un? (*Alf glowers again. Wally starts to add milk bill — stops*) Oh, by the way. . .d'you want any cheap fags?

MIKE   How much?

WALLY   Twenty for half a dollar.

ELSE   I'll have a hundred.

MIKE   Me too.

RITA   You ain't got any more of them stockings left, have you, Wal?

WALLY   How many d'you want?

RITA   Four pairs?

WALLY   Right.

RITA   How much are they?

WALLY   Same price. But I tell you what — let me put 'em on an' I'll knock a bob off.

RITA   Gerroff.

WALLY   D'you want any make-up?

MIKE   Hey — just a minute.

WALLY   Don't worry — I'll get you some as well.

RITA   What's it like?

WALLY   It's good stuff. I tell you what else I got — some cheap scotch at a quid a bottle. All proprietary brands.

ELSE   A quid a bottle?

WALLY	Fell off the lorry — with the other things.
ALF	How can a bottle of scotch fall off a lorry? It'd smash.
WALLY	My mate was there and he caught it, didn't he?

(*Mike and Rita laugh*)

MIKE	Got any brandy?
WALLY	No. That's not gonna fall off the lorry till next week. But I got some men's raincoats. Fur-lined. Six quid. Going for twenty in the shops..
MIKE	I'd like to see one.
WALLY	I'll bring one round next time. I'll get your stuff then. (*Exits*)
ELSE	Big help he is, that Wally, an he?
ALF	He'll get done one day, he will. All he's supposed to sell is milk — not stolen goods.
ELSE	Who says it's stolen?
ALF	What you talking about? Whisky a pound a bottle? Where d'you think he gets it from then?
ELSE	He told you — it falls off a lorry and his friend catches it.
ALF	How naive can you get? It's knocked off, annit? Nicked. It's out of your warehouses, annit? That's where he gets all that stuff from.
ELSE	I don't care where it comes from. Anyway, it's cheap.
MIKE	Don't ask questions an' you can't get involved.
ALF	Typical! Typical, annit, of your welfare state? Something for nothing, annit? It's the job of every responsible citizen to co-operate with the police, they keep asking you. You turn a blind eye, you're accessory after yer fact, any lawyer'll tell you that. (*Exits to hall*)

(*Wally enters front door*)

WALLY	How many?
ALF	Two.

(*Wally gives him two bottles of scotch — and goes*)

ALF	(*to himself*) Well, if I didn't somebody else would.

SCENE 4	The living-room: later that evening. Alf is still trying to paper the living-room.
ALF	Yer million unemployed, that's what I'm talking about..
MIKE	Lies! Lies!
ALF	Caused as a consequence of his Selective Employment Tax.
MIKE	Whose?

ALF Your darlin' Harold — that's whose. He's clobbered the firms for that twenty-five bob per person per week — put a million out of work over it — an' now he's got to pay that million unemployed ten pound a week each dole money. I mean, there ain't even no sense in it, is there? I mean, he's grabbed it in with one hand and now he's got to pay out ten times as much with the other. An' you call him a bloody economist. I wouldn't trust him with a jamjar of threepenny bits. And another little thing too. What's that million unemployed going to be doing all day, eh? What are *they* going to be up to? Blimey, talk about the population explosion — they'll be breeding like rabbits, they will. An' that's gonna cost him more money, annit? With children's allowances. . .an' free orange juice' an all that. . .

MIKE (*ad libbing against this*) Look, wait a minute, wait a minute. . .

ALF Blimey, your doctors'll want overtime for delivering all them babies.

ELSE (*idly cutting patterns out of a piece of wallpaper*) And your midwives.

ALF Yeah, and then we'll have to have another bloody war then to get rid of a few of 'em. (*To Mike*) Where's that bit I cut to fit up there?

MIKE (*holds up piece of paper*) Is this it?

ALF No. It's about this size. (*Demonstrates*)

ELSE (*holds up cut-out*) Look!

ALF You silly moo! That's the piece!

MIKE   Look, there isn't any free orange juice now — your lot — your Tories — put the block on that, mate.

RITA   Yer, one of the meanest things they ever done, that was. Making people pay one an' six for a bottle of orange juice.

ALF   Well, that's their own fault, annit? I mean, they wanna go around having loads of kids — let 'em buy their own orange juice. I mean, they want the pleasure of having 'em — let 'em pay the price. We wan't greedy we wasn't, me an' your mum — we stuck with one. If we'd have wanted to, we could have gone around and filled the house with the patter of tiny feet...

ELSE   (*sniffs*) Huh.

ALF   But we had a bit of planning, we did.

ELSE   Planning? It wasn't so much planning — you always seemed to be too drunk to do anything.

ALF   Look...

ELSE   It's a miracle we had *her*, you ask me.

ALF   What you talking about? Silly moo! We could have had kids if we wanted 'em!

MIKE   So you're not the old stag you try an' make out to be, eh?

ALF   Look, bloody Shirley Temple, there's nothing wrong with my virileness. You ain't had any yet, so don't you start. Long-haired pansy!

RITA   He's no pansy.

MIKE   Well, we're not ready yet. We haven't got a place of our own.

ALF   Yer...good excuse that is, annit?

ELSE   (*rises*) Look, are you going to finish this room, or stand arguing all day?

ALF   Arguing? Who's arguing? (*Pushes Mike and Rita*) Look, get out of the way, an' let's get this room done. That's the trouble with yer world today (*pasting paper*) everyone's ready to argue, but nobody's ready to do anything.

ELSE   Hark who's talking!

ALF   It's true, annit? You've got every country at each other country's throat...none of your Churches can agree. I mean, you got so many religions now you don't know where you are. An' they can't all be right, can they? I mean, according to the book there's only one true one, so the rest of 'em's lying, ain't they?

ELSE   Belong to your own, that's the only way.

ALF   It's not a question of your own is it? Eh? It's a question of His, annit? What one does He belong to?

ELSE   Who?

ALF   (*points at ceiling*) Him — Him up there — yer God! That's the one you got to belong to. No good belonging to any of the others. But who knows which one is His? I mean, that's your problem, annit? 'Cos God ain't said nothing for years, He ain't.

MIKE   Perhaps He's not up there any more.

ALF   What you talking about?

MIKE   He might have died, mightn't He?

ALF   Don't talk bloody stupid, you — Look, how can He die, you great hairy Nellie? You can't die up in Heaven. It's down here, this is the only place you can die. Can't die up there. Trouble is, you can belong to a religion all your life, support it properly, give money to it, an' when you die, you get up there and find out it was the wrong one, an' the one round the corner was the right one. . .or something. I mean, that's what's so perplexing for all us mortals down here.

ELSE   (*comes up to Alf who is now on chair by kitchen door*) Wait a minute.

ALF   What?

ELSE   I want to get out.

ALF   Well, can't you wait till I've finished?

ELSE   No, I'm bursting.

ALF   Gawd — blimey — annit marvellous? (*Gets down and lets her leave the room*)

MIKE   You ought to join all of the religions — don't take any chances. . .

ALF   (*gets back on chair*) What you mean, join all of 'em? Don't be daft. How can you join all of 'em?

RITA   It'd cost you a few bob.

ALF   I mean, He ought to give some indication to us. I mean, He wants us, don't He? (*Points*) He wants us up there. . .

(*Else opens door and tugs his jacket*)

ALF (*looks down*) Oh blimey, *now* what do you want?

ELSE I want to come in a minute.

ALF What for?

ELSE Mind your own business.

(*He gets down again*)

ALF Come on, bloody nuisance...

(*Else enters the room. While Alf climbs back onto chair, she puts on cardigan, then tugs at him again*)

ELSE I want to go out again.

ALF Cor blimey — what did you come back in for?

ELSE (*indicates cardigan*) For this...it's parky out there.

ALF Well, wait till I've finished this. Blimey, what's wrong with this paper?

ELSE You cut it too short.

ALF Blimey, how can you work like this? Look, clear off the lot of you — go on...

ELSE Alright. I'll go round to me sister's — an' I won't come back till you've finished. Pig!

ALF Don't come back!

ELSE Don't worry, I won't. (*Exits*)

RITA (*to Mike*) Come on, let's go to the pictures. Let him do it himself, miserable old perisher.

MIKE Yer. (*Points to Heaven*) You ought to try an' get Him to come down an' give you a hand. He made the world in seven days — blimey, He'd do this in a couple of minutes.

ALF (*lunges at him with paste brush*) Gerroff! You scouse git!

(*Mike and Rita run out and shut the door. Alf stands in room on his own. He hears street door slam. He comes down to table*)

ALF (*starts to paste up paper*) He did, though. (*Awestruck*) Made the world in seven days...blimey, the whole world — England, America, Russia, China — cor! Not counting all them stars an' things...an' the moon an' the sun. Made all of them in the same week, too, He did. Blimey, He didn't hang about — must have been hard at it all week. Not like some of 'em today...some of the rubbish you get now...in the bog smoking all day. (*Pastes in silence for a while*) Miracle. He could come down here, do this room out, sort all the world out, He could, all our problems, an' be back up there by tea time. Wonder why He don't? Not interested — not bothered, I suppose. (*Pause*) Perhaps He don't know. You'd think people would tell Him though...I mean, there's thousands of 'em going up there every day...you'd think some of them would tell Him...tell Him the state we're in down here. (*Pause*) Still, probably too busy — big place, Heaven, annit? I mean, it's a lot for one God. (*He holds paper up and stands on chair placing foot on paper — puts*

other foot on paper — lifts paper — it tears again. Lifts his eyes to Heaven) Oh God, what have I done to deserve this, why me? They're all right, an they? They've all gone out. She's gone to her sister's. They've gone to the pictures — I got to stay and do this. I could have gone to football, God. The Hammers are playing at home this afternoon — I suppose you know that anyway. But I'll show 'em. I'll paper this room out if it's the last thing I do. (*Realises what he's said*) It won't be though, God, will it? Please?

SCENE 5   **The living-room: some days later.**

ALF (*looking round room admiringly*) Well, that's not bad — not bad at all, though I say it myself, not bad.

MAN That'll be eight and a half quid.

ALF *Eight and a half*! You said five!

MAN Well, I had to strip off the old paper, didn't I? And you don't want your missus to know I did it, do you?

(*Alf counts out all the money he has and pays up. Man exits*)

ELSE (*meets man in hall*) Hello, what are you doing here?

MAN Come to see the room Alf's papered. Marvellous job he's made there, marvellous. (*Exits*)

(*Else enters room. She looks round it. Alf watches her*)

ALF (*proudly*) Well? What d'you think then, eh?

ELSE (*looks round the room again, studying it. Finally she speaks*) I don't know. . .I don't know if I like it.

ALF	Eh? You picked the paper!
ELSE	I know, but I don't think I like it, not now it's up. No, I think I prefer it as it was.
ALF	You silly moo! Right! That's the last thing I do in this house. (*Lunges at door*)
ELSE	Where you going?
ALF	Up the pub!

(*Else walks around the room looking at new paper. Alf re-enters and sits down miserably*)

ELSE	I thought you were going up the pub.
ALF	I haven't got any money, have I?

The Funeral

Till Death Us Do Part: No. 4 (3rd Series)

Recording: 14th January 1968

Transmission: 26th January 1968

The Funeral

SCENE 1　The Garnetts' living-room. It is still daylight, but the room is very gloomy. Alf sits in chair, looking noble and dignified. Else sits in chair, looking very serious. Mike and Rita sit on the sofa, looking bored. Rita looks at Mike. Mike shrugs — he looks at Else. Else looks prim. Alf looks self-righteous. Rita, bored, leans on Mike, then looks at Else. Else looks prim. Alf still looks self-righteous.

MIKE　I think it's bloody daft, you ask me.

ALF　No one's asking you, are they?

RITA　(*groaning*) Oh, Gordon Bennett! But it's so silly!

ELSE　I don't care. Silly or not, I don't think we should have the telly on tonight. Not with poor old Mrs Weatherby laying dead across the road.

MIKE　Well, I can't see how it can bother her — she can't hear it, can she?

ALF　Ain't you got no respect? Eh? Scouse git! That's the trouble with your modern generation — got no respect for nothing, they ain't!

RITA　You're marvellous, you are, ain't you? You're marvellous. When she was alive you didn't have a good word to say for her. But now she's dead, you're so full of respect!

ALF　Look. . .

ELSE　I've heard you speak against her.

ALF　Look — alright, I may have said the odd word. Might have made the odd remark. I mean, no one's perfect. And she had her faults alright, didn't she?

ELSE　She wasn't that bad.

ALF　I'm not saying she was, am I? I mean, there's some down this street a lot worse than her. I mean, I know that.

ELSE　Rude to her, you was. Rude to her face, sometimes.

ALF Look, I might have been...but I'm wearing black for her now though, an I? Eh? (*Pointing to black armband on sleeve*) I'm wearing black for her now, an I?

ELSE Bit late, isn't it? Shutting the stable door...

ALF Which is more than *some* people down this street will do for her.

ELSE She can't see you though, can she?

MIKE (*pointing to Alf's armband*) What are you wearing that for?

ALF Token of respect for the departed.

RITA Blimey, that's going a bit far, Dad, isn't it?

MIKE You hoping to get invited to the wake or something?

ALF What you talking about?

MIKE Well, there's bound to be a booze-up after the funeral, isn't there? There usually is round this way.

RITA Yeah. Weddings, funerals and christenings — they're all a good excuse for a booze-up round here. The last funeral Dad went to, me and Mum had to help him up the stairs when he got home, and put him to bed.

ELSE Kicked me, he did.

MIKE I know. My old man prefers a wake to a wedding. He says (*Irish brogue*) 'seeing a man off on his way to Heaven is no occasion to be unhappy'.

RITA Oh, come on, let's have the telly on. It's bad enough having the blinds drawn all day, but it's ridiculous sitting like this. I mean, it's not as though it's a relation or anything. She was only a neighbour.

ALF That's no reason why you shouldn't show a bit of respect, is it?

MIKE Respect?

ALF Yer, respect, you scouse git!

RITA Well, *you* show the respect and let *us* have the telly on! You needn't watch it — you can turn your chair round the other way.

MIKE Or better still, let us take it upstairs and watch it in our room.

ALF Look, that's my telly an' it's staying where it is.

RITA (*listening at the wall*) Next door have got theirs on.

ALF I'm not surprised at nothing they do in there. She didn't even wear black when his sister died. His own sister!

ELSE That was 'cos of him, that was. That was his fault. She told me herself. She said he wouldn't wear black for her mother, so why should she wear black for his sister? He said he couldn't afford black for her mother. But as soon as it's his side of the family, it's different. He can afford it then. Upset about that, she was, 'cos she was fond of his sister. It was the only one in his family she liked.

(*Pause*)

MIKE   (*to Alf*) You'll miss the football.

ALF   What football?

MIKE   It's West Ham on the telly tonight.

ELSE   She was sitting crying over the corner shop this afternoon. . .

ALF   Who they playing?

ELSE   Saying how upset she was. . .about Mrs Weatherby. . .

MIKE   Fulham.

ELSE   She's soon got over it, ain't she?

ALF   Bound to beat them, then. Johnny Haynes and his bloody seven dwarfs. . .

ELSE   Sitting in there enjoying herself now. . .watching telly. . .

MIKE   You gonna watch it, then?

ELSE   I thought then she was making more out of it than she needed to. . .

ALF   Dunno. . .I mean. . .

ELSE   She didn't even draw her curtains till I drew mine.

ALF   I mean, people go by and hear the telly on. . .I mean, they'll think we're as bad as them next door.

RITA All you're worried about is what other people might think.

MIKE Turn the sound off. No one will hear it with the sound off. All you'll miss is Kenneth Wolstenholme's commentary. And who wants to hear that? The cobblers he spouts!

ALF Like to see 'em. Like to see the Hammers. (*Looks at Else*)

(*There is a pause. Mike looks at Else. Rita looks at Else*)

ELSE Don't look at me.

ALF Well, I mean...wouldn't hurt, would it? With the sound off, I mean. Be no sound on...

ELSE I'll leave it to your own conscience.

ALF Well, look, I mean...I've done a lot for her, an I? I mean, after what I've done for her...(*Else reacts*) I mean, she wouldn't begrudge me watching football, would she? I mean, with the sound off, as well.

RITA What've you done for her? What did you ever do for her?

ALF I've done my bit, don't you worry.

ELSE Your dad's organized a collection for her. To give her a send-off.

RITA To give her a send-off!

ALF Yer, well, I mean — she's an old-age pensioner, ain't she? Got no relations or anything...I mean...don't wanna go to the cemetery on her own, do she?

MIKE Eh?

ALF Well, only decent, annit? Give her a proper send-off...I mean, she's lived down the street over forty years, ain't she?

RITA So you've organized a collection for her? And what does the money get spent on?

ALF To give her a decent funeral. (*Mike and Rita can't believe their ears*) I mean, people round this way set a lot on that sort of thing. I mean, the way you go — it's important, annit? I mean, they save up for it — take out insurance, don't they, to guard against it.

MIKE Guard against what?

ALF Not having a proper send-off!!!

MIKE Gawd! Annit marvellous, eh? They're the same up in Liverpool — they don't give tuppence how you live, as long as you get a decent ride to the cemetery.

ALF Look...

MIKE It's tragic, annit, when you think about it? I mean, there's a poor old pensioner, living on her own, struggling to live on four and a half quid a week, and the only time anybody does anything for her is when she's dead. You ask 'em to do anything for her while she's alive — oh no. Too much trouble.

ELSE   I done things for her. I went over there an' cleaned for her, and cooked her meals, many times. You know that, Rita.

RITA   Yer, I know you did. And while you were over there doing it, who done all the moaning about it? (*Pointing at Alf*) Him! If he came home and found his tea wasn't ready because you were helping out over there, he went potty. And now he's organizing collections for her!

ALF   Look, someone had to do it, didn't they? An' it's no bloody fun going round asking people for money! Annit marvellous, eh? Annit marvellous? You do someone a good turn, an' all you get is sneered at.

MIKE   A good turn?

ALF   Look, you wouldn't understand, would you? You wouldn't understand them things — you ignorant lout! I bet if either of us went — me or Mummy here — if either of us went, and we had to rely on you two to bury us, we'd end up in a bloody council coffin!

ELSE   I don't need anyone to bury *me*. I can bury myself. I've got me own insurance for that.

ALF   So have I. And we're gonna need it, with them two.

RITA   Oh give over, Dad. Blimey, what a subject to talk about.

ALF   Well, got to be faced, annit?

RITA   Stop it! You're not going yet, either of you.

ALF   (*looking at Else*) Hope not...but —

MIKE   I can't understand this fascination for funerals, myself. I mean, when I go, I don't care how they send me. I won't be here, will I? It won't concern me.

ALF   It won't concern me, either! Ignorant swine! You've got no respect for nothing, you ain't. No respect at all.

MIKE   Look, I've got respect for *life*, I have — not bloody death. Anyway, you going to watch the football?

ALF   No! An' neither are you, either. Not on my television.

MIKE   Aagh — stick your television!

(*Alf glares. Mike glares back. There is a long pause*)

ELSE   I ordered the ham.

RITA   Ham?

ELSE   For afterwards.

RITA   After what?

ELSE   The funeral. I mean, they'll want a bite to eat afterwards.

RITA   Who?

ELSE The people who go. I've told 'em all to come back here.

ALF Yer.

ELSE I thought it would be better to come back here. Well, they don't want to go back to a cold, empty house, do they? It'll be more cheerful here. I mean, it'll be warmer. There'll be a fire here.

MIKE Hey! Who's having that house now she's gone, then?

ALF Oh! Oh! 'Who's going to have the house now she's gone?' He's the one what was all concerned about her, wasn't he? But she's not even been put down yet, an' he's after her house already. Typical that is, annit? Typical!

RITA They're selling it.

MIKE D'you enquire, then?

RITA Mum did.

ELSE Yes, I went to see Chapman the landlords, an' they said they wasn't interested in renting any more. They wanna sell. They're selling 'em all up round here, as soon as people get out. (*There is a knock at the door*) That's Mr Williams from the corner shop. He said he'd bring the ham across when he'd cut it. (*She exits to answer the door*)

MIKE Hmm, I wonder how much they'll want for it?

ALF What's it matter? I mean, blimey, whatever they want for it you can't bloody well afford it. You ain't got no money, have yer?

(*Else returns with Mr Williams*)

MR WILLIAMS   Evening. (*Turns to Mike and Rita*) Good evening. (*He gives the ham to Else and looks at Alf*) Sorry business, all this, annit?

ALF   Yer. Still, it happens to us all.

MR WILLIAMS   Yer. S'pose so. Not done *me* no good, though, her going like that — so sudden.

ALF   Eh, What do you mean?

MR WILLIAMS   Well, she went owing me a few bob.

ALF   That's a nice thing to say, annit?

MR WILLIAMS   Not saying nothing...

ALF   A fine time to talk, annit? I mean, to bring that up now, maligning the woman, now she's gone.

MR WILLIAMS   Not maligning her. All I said, she went owing me a few bob, that's all. That's all I said.

ALF   Well, she couldn't bloody well help that. I mean, blimey, it's not her fault she went, is it?

MR WILLIAMS   Not saying that...

ALF   I mean, she didn't go on purpose just to do you out of a few bob, did she?

MR WILLIAMS   Not saying that, am I? All I'm saying, if she'd gone on Saturday instead of Wednesday, I'd have been alright. 'Cos she always paid me Fridays, you see.

ALF   Look, I don't suppose she *wanted* to go on Wednesday. I mean, blimey, if she'd had her way, I should think she'd have preferred to stay till Saturday...

ELSE Or even longer.

ALF I mean, blimey, she had no bloody choice, mate.

MR WILLIAMS Not saying that. Just saying, that's all, it's cost me money. Her going Wednesday, that's all. Still, just my luck, I s'pose.

ALF Just *your* luck? What about *her* bloody luck?

MR WILLIAMS Not saying that. All I'm saying. . .not blaming her. . .I mean, she was a good payer. . .always was. All I'm saying — there's no one left, you see. I mean, if she had relations. . .someone left. . .to sort of clear things up for her, I'd have been better off, that's all. That's all I'm

saying. But there ain't no one, you see, so it's me who's the loser. That's all I'm saying.

ALF (*explodes*) Well, bloody hard luck, annit?

MR WILLIAMS Well, it is in a way, annit? I mean, it wasn't only one week. She owed two, you know. I mean, another thing, the street's having a whip round, annit? I mean, to give her a good send-off, like.

ALF Well?

MR WILLIAMS I ain't saying nothing bad about that. I mean, I've put in meself! I mean, you know that. Well....

ALF *Well?*

MR WILLIAMS Well, they're buying things, ain't they? You know, flowers...an' other things...I mean, ham (*indicates parcel*) an'...other things — you know. To give her a good send-off, like. You know...

ALF   Yer.

MR WILLIAMS   Well, I mean — all I'm saying is, no one's thought — no one's give a thought, none of the organizers, I mean... None of 'em's give a thought about paying her bills for the stuff she had before — you know. That's all I'm saying...that's all I'm saying. That's all.

ELSE   Hmm, see what you mean.

MR WILLIAMS   Yer. That's what I'm saying.

ELSE   Yer, see what you mean.

MR WILLIAMS   Yer — that's what I'm saying.

ELSE   Hm. (*To Alf*) See what he means.

ALF   *I* see what he means, too! He wants us to bung him out of the send-off money. That's what he means.

MR WILLIAMS   Well...I mean, everyone else has had their money, ain't they? Undertakers, an' the flowers people. They'll get theirs alright. An' the pub — they'll get theirs, too.

ALF   You'll get yours for the ham.

MR WILLIAMS   Oh yer. For *this*, yer. But only for this. Not for the other. I mean, I'm the loser on that...on the other stuff she had — on the groceries before she went.

ALF   That ain't my fault, is it?

MR WILLIAMS   Not saying that...

ALF   What are you telling me for, then?

MR WILLIAMS   Well, who else should I tell? I mean, you organized the fund, didn't you? I mean, you're in charge of the money that's been collected, aren't you?

ALF   Look, that money's for her send-off, annit? I mean, that's what people's donated that for, annit?

MR WILLIAMS   Yer, I know that.

ELSE   I think Mr Williams ought to be paid. (*Mr Williams nods approvingly*) I don't think she'd want to go with that on her conscience. (*He shakes his head in agreement*) Lovely bit of ham...I'm sure she'd want Mr Williams to be paid.

MR WILLIAMS   (*nods in agreement*) She would — oh, she would, I'm sure she would

ELSE   So am I.

MR WILLIAMS   (*nodding*) I mean, that kind of woman, wasn't she?

(*Rita pulls a face at Mike. He responds with a similar sickly grimace*)

ELSE   (*nods in agreement*) Yes. She was. You're right.

MR WILLIAMS   I know.

ELSE   (*to Alf*) I'm sure she wouldn't like to think Mr Williams hadn't been paid. She wouldn't rest if she thought that.

ALF Yer, but that's not the point, is it? I mean, you're right. I agree with you. I'm sure she'd want him to be paid. But it's not her money, is it? That's the problem. It's other people's money, annit? And they donated that money to give her a good send-off — not to pay her grocery bills. (*To Mr Williams*) You'd better go round and ask *them*. 'Cos the only things I'm authorized to spend that money on is. . .

MIKE Booze.

ALF An' flowers! An' flowers!

(*Mr Williams looks at Else. Else looks at Alf*)

MR WILLIAMS (*almost in tears*) Just my luck, annit? Just my luck. Things ain't bad enough, people have to die owing me money. (*Starts to leave*)

ELSE There's a lot of things in her cupboard still, Mr Williams — tins of things she hadn't used. I mean, if they came from you. . .I mean, you could take 'em back, I suppose.

MR WILLIAMS Yer, I could do that, I suppose.

ELSE I've got the keys if you want to go over there. (*She goes to get them*)

MR WILLIAMS No, no, I won't go now. I'll wait till after the funeral — show a bit of respect. Goodnight.

ELSE Goodnight. Let me know when you want to get in there.

MR WILLIAMS The ham came to twelve shillings and sixpence. (*Exits*)

ALF Bloody marvellous, annit, eh? Expecting the street to pay his bad debts. I mean, blimey, she was a good customer of his, she was.

ELSE She bought nearly everything off him.

MIKE I feel sorry for him, myself. He's a dying race, he is.

ALF Talking about? He's English, the same as us.

MIKE I'm talking about his living. The corner shopkeeper. They're dying out. They're being absorbed by the big supermarkets. It's progress, but you can still feel sorry for him.

ALF Supermarket? Progress? Don't talk daft. Progress!

MIKE It is progress, isn't it? I mean, blimey, even *you* can't argue with that.

ALF How's it progress, then?

MIKE Well, of course it is. It's a more efficient means of distribution, isn't it?

ALF Efficient? What are you talking about, efficient? I mean, blimey, your supermarket is a prime example of your bloody Labour inefficiency, if you ask me.

MIKE Eh?

RITA He's potty.

ALF Never mind about potty. I mean, you go in them places — supermarkets — you've got to bloody serve yourself, haven't you?

Eh? They don't attempt to serve you, do they? Oh no. I mean, *you're* working for *them*. All they want to do is sit by the till on their backsides and take your money.

MIKE (*laughing*) But that *is* more efficient. It's modern methods.

ALF Modern methods!

RITA And it's quicker.

MIKE Better service.

ALF Quicker? Better service? Blimey! Talking about? Eh? I mean, you buy one thing. You manage to find that — an' then the next thing you want is bloody miles away, at the end of the shop.

RITA Oh, I see. I suppose you want to stay with Mr Williams and the corner shop, do you?

ALF Yer, well? What's wrong with it?

ELSE It's handy.

MIKE What's wrong with it? It's bloody filthy for a start. That's what's wrong with it.

ALF Yer? Well, one thing about Mr Williams, mate — you can get a bit of tick there. I mean, if you're an old-age pensioner you can get a bit of credit. But I mean, you go up your supermarket and try an' get a dozen eggs on the slate till Friday and see what they say.

ELSE Or a packet of tea.

RITA Mr Williams' shop! It's awful in there!

ALF Talking about — awful?

RITA It's not hygienic, that's what I'm talking about. Flies, there are — all over his bacon.

ALF Flies? A few flies won't hurt you, my dear, will they? At least his bacon's got a bit of taste, annit?

ELSE He brushes his flies off it.

ALF (*scoffing*) Not hygienic!

ELSE He don't let 'em stay on it.

MIKE Look, you go to the supermarket and everything is under cover. And the bacon is hermetically sealed, in hygienic plastic bags.

ALF So it might be, mate. (*Points at Else*) But she goes up there — she goes up there an' buys it, an' she brings it home, don't she, eh? An' she opens it. . .she undoes your hermeygenic seals. . .and *then* the bloody flies get on it.

ELSE They'd be *our* flies, though.

ALF What are you talking about? It don't matter whose bloody flies they are, do it?

ELSE   Well, if they're our flies, we know where they've been, don't we?

ALF   What are you talking about? Silly moo! 'Our flies'! They could be anybody's flies, couldn't they? They could be next door's flies for all we know. And who knows *where* they've been? I mean, blimey, you can't have your own bloody flies. Flies ain't like mice. You can have your own mice, but you can't have your own bloody flies. I mean, they're too mobile, flies, an they? They come in through windows an' things. They ain't like mice.

ELSE   Them mice are not ours anyway.

ALF   Not the point.

ELSE   They come in from next door too.

ALF   Well, you can't blame 'em, can you? You leave too much out for 'em. I mean, blimey, the way you carry on, it's a wonder we ain't got every mouse in the street living here. Bloody welfare state for mice, this house is.

ELSE   Look, if you blocked the holes up, they couldn't get in.

ALF   An' if you kept the house a bit neat and tidy, an' put things away proper, they wouldn't want to!

ELSE   Pig!

ALF   Belt up, great ragbag! (*Else reacts*) Anyway, supermarkets. . .

RITA   (*getting up*) I've heard enough from you tonight. I'm going to bed.

MIKE   (*rises too*) Me too.

(*They go to the door*)

ALF   (*jeering*) That's it! That's it! You can't win argument — go to bed. Typical that is, annit? That's typical, that is. When you're bested — go to bed. . .

(*Mike and Rita exit*)

SCENE 2   Mike and Rita's bedroom. Mike and Rita enter.

MIKE   Bloody old fool.

RITA   He's awful some nights, isn't he? The way he speaks to Mum — I don't know how she puts up with it. (*She sits on the bed*)

MIKE   (*putting his arm round her and kissing her*) Hm. . .never mind. Mmmm, let's go to bed.

RITA   (*kissing him back*) Mmm. . .

(*They kiss for a while, then Rita breaks away*)

RITA   I wonder if *we'll* ever get like them?

MIKE   No. . .

RITA They couldn't have always been like that, I'm sure. Perhaps that's the way all marriages go. Perhaps everyone gets like that?

MIKE *(kisses her)* Not us.

RITA They can't love each other any more. You know — not the way people should. They've got feelings for each other, I suppose, a sort of attachment, but it's not love.

MIKE *(still kissing her)* The passion's gone.

RITA All Dad thinks about is beer and football — and Mum, I don't even think she thinks at all. *(Pushes Mike away slightly)* D'you think it might happen to us?

MIKE No...no, we're different.

(From downstairs comes the sound of football on TV: roars from the crowds and the voice of the commentator)

COMMENTATOR And as West Ham go one up...

(Mike breaks away and rushes to bedroom door)

RITA Where are you going?

MIKE He's put the football on! *(Exits)*

(Rita hurls shoe at the door)

SCENE 3 The living-room: after the funeral. Food and drink are set out on the table. Mike pours himself a large scotch as Rita enters, carrying a plate of sandwiches.

RITA They should be back soon.

MIKE *(looking out of window)* Here they are now.

(The door opens: Alf and Else enter with Gran. They are followed by neighbours. They sit down)

ELSE Here you are. Sit down, Gran. What are you going to have?

GRAN A little drop of gin'll do me.

FIRST MAN *(asks for drinks)*

(Alfs pours out drinks helped by Mike and Rita)

ALF	Well, cheers! (*Drinks*) Aah! Went alright, eh? Today – seemed to go alright, didn't it?
SECOND MAN	Yer, went smooth enough.
ALF	Yer, went well. Pleased about that. Pleased it went alright for her.
FIRST MAN	Yer, went alright.
SECOND MAN	Bit fast.
ELSE	Yer – he got a bit of speed up after he got out of the street, didn't he?
MR WILLIAMS	Yer. One of the fastest funerals I've ever been to.
GRAN	I prefer the horses, meself.
ELSE	Yer, I know – they don't use them any more, do they?
GRAN	I prefer them. Sooner have horses, myself.
ALF	(*shouting*) They don't have 'em any more!

GRAN	*(nods)* Hm...yes.
ALF	*(shakes head)* No!
GRAN	*(nods)* Hm. Yes.
ALF	Oh Gawd. No! *They don't have 'em any more*!
GRAN	*(nods)* That's right. Four — four to each coach, they was...
ALF	*(aside to man)* Silly old faggot. I don't know what she bothered to come back for, meself.
MAN	*(grins)* Yer...
ALF	Could have done two for the price of one.

 (Mr Williams glares)

GRAN	*(to Else)* I don't want to go in a car.
ELSE	No.
GRAN	Prefer the horses, meself — four black horses.
ELSE	*(nods)* Yes.
GRAN	Funerals ain't what they used to be, are they? I remember, when my mother went — Gawd rest her soul — it was a lovely funeral when she went. Everyone down the street all said it was the best funeral they'd ever seen. All the neighbours lined the streets, they did. An' they didn't start the horses trotting, they didn't break into a trot, until they was four streets away, they didn't.
ELSE	I know, different now. They just rush you off now.
GRAN	Eh?
ELSE	I said, they can't get you down fast enough, now.
GRAN	She laid in the house for nearly a week before they screwed her down. And all the men took turns to sit through the night with her. Ah, yes. Yes. It's all different now. They ain't the same — funerals ain't what they used to be. *(Wipes her eyes, holds up glass)* D'you think I could have a drop more gin, please?
ELSE	Yes, of course. *(To Alf)* Drop of gin for Gran, please. *(Alf pours her a gin)* She likes a large one. *(Alf, glaring, pours a large one)*
ALF	*(raising his own glass)* Well, it's a sad occasion, I know, but we mustn't be too downhearted, I s'pose. In the midst of life there is...

 (Gran starts to cry in her gin)

ELSE	Never mind, Gran, never mind.
GRAN	She was...she was a good woman.
ELSE	Who — Mrs Weatherby? Yes...
GRAN	No — my Mum.
ALF	*(to Else)* Shut her up! Her and her bloody mother. We're not here for

	her mother, are we? (*To neighbours*) No, as I was saying, like...it's a sad loss. But she'd be very pleased, I think, if she could have seen how we sent her off today.
OMNES	Hear, hear.
ALF	I mean, so...what I mean is, we mustn't be too downhearted 'cos...I mean, after all...I mean, she was no youngster.
MR WILLIAMS	No, that's true.
GRAN	(*breaks down*) Why'd they have to take her? There's all the villains in the world! Why'd they have to take her? Eh? *Why?*
ALF	Look — she was ninety-one!
GRAN	She wasn't — she was only eighty.
ELSE	No, Mrs Weatherby was ninety-one, Gran.
GRAN	I'm not talking about her, I'm talking about my Mum.
ALF	(*to Else*) Look, can't you keep her quiet? She's spoiling everything, she is.
RITA	Shut up, Dad!
ALF	Well, I mean, it's got nothing to do with her Mum, this ain't. (*To neighbours*) No...as I was saying, they always say that they give 'em a good send-off down Tinto Road, but I reckon, speaking personally, meself, Tinto Road can't hold a candle to this street.
MAN	Hear, hear.
ALF	I mean, what we done today, I reckon (*indicates food and drink*) I mean, the spread an' that, I mean, I don't think Tinto Road does as well as that.
MAN	No...you done well there, Alf. I mean, on the money, you done well on the money.
MR WILLIAMS	She went owing me a few bob...
ALF	Well, I ain't one to boast, but...(*Gran starts to sing one of the old songs. They all look at her*) Cor blimey, she thinks she's at a bloody wedding now.
ELSE	Oh, leave her alone, she's enjoying herself.
ALF	But she's not s'posed to, is she? Not s'posed to be here to bloody enjoy herself, is she?
ELSE	Mrs Weatherby wouldn't mind her singing, so I don't see what it's got to do with you.
ALF	Look, how do you know what Mrs Weatherby would mind or not mind? Eh? (*Points to Gran*) An' how would she like it, if someone was to sing at her funeral, eh?
ELSE	I'll sing at yours. Pig!
ALF	Oh yer? Yer? Look, you wanna make sure you don't go first, mate!

RITA Dad!

ELSE I'll dance on your grave, don't you worry. (*She starts to sing with Gran*)

(*Alf tries to continue his speech. Everyone starts singing with Gran. Alf is forced to give in and ostentatiously joins in the singing*)

Women's Lib. and Bournemouth

Till Death Us Do Part: No. 5 (4th Series)

Recording: 27th August 1972

Transmission: 27th September 1972

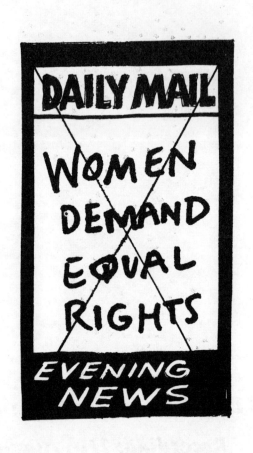

Woman's Lib. and Bournemouth

SCENE 1   The Garnetts' living-room: evening. Else is ironing underwear. Rita is busy sorting out summer clothes. Alf and Mike are both stretched out reading.

RITA   (*looking at swimming costume*) I wonder if we'll get any decent weather?

MIKE   We've not had much so far. We should have gone to Spain like I said.

ALF   Well, we ain't going to Spain, are we? You wanna go to Spain – you go to bloody Spain. We're going to Bournemouth.

MIKE   Yeah, an' sit an' bloody freeze.

ALF   Yer, well, it'll be better than sitting in Spain covered in bloody flies, won't it? Spain! Bloody filthy out there, it is.

ELSE   It'll suit you then.

ALF   Eh? What're you on about?

ELSE   (*holds up Alf's long johns*) These. It's took me nearly all day to get these clean.

ALF   (*reacts*) Look. . .

ELSE	You're worse to wash for than the baby is.
ALF	Look...
ELSE	They advertise on the telly...
ALF	Look...
ELSE	All them washing powders —
ALF	Listen...
ELSE	Miracle cleaners — biological stains —
ALF	Shurrup!
ELSE	The washing powder ain't been invented that'll remove *his* stains. I've scrubbed these till I've almost worn 'em out. He wears 'em a fortnight before he'll change 'em — that's the trouble. The dirt's ground in 'em, it is.

(*Alf tries to ignore her*)

RITA	I know. You don't have to tell me, I've washed 'em myself.
ELSE	(*looking pointedly at Alf*) It's not ordinary dirt, either.
ALF	Shurrup!
ELSE	Well, it's not so bad at home, but if he wears these in the hotel, what will people think?
MIKE	They'll think he's dirty, that's all.
ALF	Shurrup you — nothing to do with you!
ELSE	I mean, he sleeps in 'em.
RITA	Look, Dad, why don't you buy some pyjamas? Just to wear at Bournemouth.
ALF	Look, I'm not dressing up for no bloody hotels. Getting all dolled up just to go to bed — bloody daft, that is.

MIKE   He can borrow a pair of mine if he likes.

ALF   I don't want to borrow a pair of yours. I'm a bit fussy about what I sleep in.

RITA   *(points at long johns)* Those?

ALF   Look, if the Maker had wanted us to wear pyjamas, we'd have been born in 'em.

ELSE   *(holds up long johns again)* You wasn't born in these either, was you?

ALF   Look, everyone used to wear them in the old days. Even yer aristocracy wore 'em.

ELSE   Perhaps they did. But I bet they changed 'em more often than you change yours.

ALF   Look, I'm not wearing no pyjamas...not for you...or hotels...or anyone. I'm not going around putting on no side — I am what I am, an' that's what I'm gonna be. And any dirt that's found on me, or what I wear, is honest dirt.

ELSE   Well, I don't care how honest your dirt is, I don't like spending all day scrubbing it off these. And I don't suppose the hotel people will want it ruining their bed sheets either.

ALF   Look, we're paying to stay there, ain't we? Eh? They're not taking us in out of the goodness of their heart, are they?

ELSE   I know we're paying. But that's no reason for behaving like a pig, is it?

ALF   Look, no need to worry. I'll behave there the same way as I behave here...

ELSE   That's what I'm afraid of.

ALF   Look, I've been in bloody hotels before, you know, I wasn't dragged up. *(Else sniffs)* And when you stay in hotels there's no rules about what you've got to wear in bed. *(Leans forward to Mike)* If you want to go to bed dressed up like a Peruvian Ponce, you can. An' if you don't want to, you don't have to. I mean, blimey, it's not the army we're going into. You ain't got to stand by your beds an' be inspected.

ELSE   Well, I hope no one sees you wearing these, that's all.

ALF   Who's going to see me? Eh? I mean, blimey, the only one who's going to see me in bed is you, an' you've seen me often enough.

ELSE   Too often.

ALF   See, you can't have a proper discussion with her — not without her getting personal. I mean, you'd think civilized people...you'd think we'd be able to talk without picking holes in each other. I mean, that's your Woman's Lib for you, that is. In the old days, when a woman married a man, it was for better or for worse — and bloody grateful she was not to be left on the shelf. I mean, when I married *her*, she was lucky to get me — an' she knew it...an' was thankful. *(Points to television)* It's that thing I blame it on. Before that came in the house, she didn't know nothing. She was ignorant — an' better off for it. That's what's unsettled her — sitting in front of that all day — letting them stuff her head full of nonsense. *(Else sniffs)*

RITA   *(busy packing suitcases)* If men like you had their way, women would just be

	lackeys, wouldn't they? Slaves! Waiting on men hand and foot. Clean the house, make the beds, cook my meals, wash my shirts...
ALF	Well, what d'you expect 'em to do? Sit about doing nothing all day? I mean, that's their bloody job, annit? Looking after their man, an' cleaning his house, an' doing for him...
ELSE	I'll do for you!
ALF	I mean, that's what he bloody marries her for, annit?
RITA	(*picks up heavy suitcase from table and dumps it on floor*) To be an unpaid skivvy!
ALF	What are you bloody talking about? 'Unpaid'? She gets her housekeeping, don't she?
ELSE	Huh!
RITA	Women weren't born just to be drudges, Dad. Women...
ALF	Look, we all have to bloody work, don't we? (*Points at Mike*) Except bloody curly locks there. And woman's job happens to be in the home, don't it?
RITA	No. Not every woman wants to be a slave to some bloody man.
ALF	Well, it's not always a question of what they want is it? I mean, women is different to men, ain't they? Eh? I mean, that's nature, that is...an' God...He made 'em different.
RITA	Not different — they...
ALF	Look, no good arguing. No argument is going to turn a cabbage into a steak, is it? God — *He* — *He* put woman here just for man, didn't He?
RITA	What?
ALF	Yer. It's in your Bible. Yer Garden of Eden — all God done there was made man — Adam. But God, see, in His infinite wisdom, realised that He couldn't expect man to run the Garden of Eden on his own. So He, God, He took a rib an' made Eve...so she could clean...an' wash up...an' look after Adam's house for him. So, you see, if it hadn't been for man, and man's need for a home help, woman wouldn't have got born at all, in the first place. (*Points at Else*) And if she was a bit bloody faster around the bloody house (*Else reacts*) perhaps my pants wouldn't be as dirty as she bloody makes 'em out to be. Because then, she might have a bit more time to wash 'em a bit more often.
ELSE	Yes, perhaps I could — if you took 'em off a bit more often, instead of living in the bloody things for a fortnight. (*Throws pants at Alf*)

SCENE 2 The London-Bournemouth train: 1st class compartment containing Alf, Else, Rita, Mike and baby, and a gentleman. There is one empty seat opposite Alf.

ALF Bloody go-slow! Ain't it marvellous, eh? This bloody train ain't hardly moved for half an hour.

RITA Oh shut up, Dad.

ALF Well, makes yer sick, dunnit? The only sunny day we've had this year, an' we've got to spend it sitting in a bloody railway carriage. (*Sees ticket collector in corridor*) Hoi! When's this bloody train gonna get a move on?

TICKET COLLECTOR I dunno.

ALF We left Waterloo an hour ago an' we ain't even passed Clapham yet. (*Points to window*) You can still see Waterloo out of here. I could walk faster.

TICKET COLLECTOR Well, why don't yer?

ALF Look, I don't want no bloody cheek out of you. I've paid my bloody fare, I have, mate — an' I expect a bit of servility. I mean, it's alright having go-slows when you're going to work. I mean, half of 'em don't mind that — lazy sods. But *we're* going on bloody holiday, mate. I mean, we're sitting here in our own time we are, not the bloody guvnors'. No bloody lunch, we ain't had — probably miss our tea as well.

TICKET COLLECTOR	They're serving tea in the buffet car.
ALF	Yer, so they might be. But if we have tea here we got to pay for it, ain't we?
TICKET COLLECTOR	Yer, of course you have. You don't expect us to give out tea for nothing, do you?
ALF	But our tea's already paid for in Bournemouth, in our hotel where we're staying.
MIKE	Look...here (*puts his hand in his pocket*) — go an' buy a cup of tea — I mean, blimey...
ALF	I don't wanna buy a cup of tea on here. If you bought one, you wouldn't be able to drink it. They see you with a cup of tea in your hand an' they start going fast, an' jumping an' jerking, so you spill it all over you. I know 'em — bloody idle Labour rubbish.
MIKE	Look, the trouble with this country is people like you — and the Tory Government — and that fat fool Heath. Just a bloody big girl he is...
ALF	Now look...
MIKE	He took on the miners first — disrupted the whole country and plunged us into candlelight for months...
ALF	That was the miners...
MIKE	That was bloody Heath!
TICKET COLLECTOR	Bloody Heath.
ALF	Look...
MIKE	And the miners clobbered him. Then he took on the railways — and lost again.
ALF	Look...
MIKE	Then he started on the dockers — and they beat him too.
TICKET COLLECTOR	An' they beat him too.
ALF	Look...
MIKE	All he's doing is driving the country nearer to bankruptcy every day, he is.
ALF	Look...
MIKE	Why don't he give *all* the workers a proper rise, an' let 'em get on with their work?
ALF	'Cos they ain't worth a bloody rise, that's why. I mean, look at him. (*Points to ticket collector*) What *does* he bloody look like? Egg all down the front of his uniform — why don't they smarten theirselves

	|up at least? I mean, what must foreigners think when they get on these trains and see the likes of him?
RITA	Hark at Beau Brummel! Blimey, you're hardly out of the pages of *Nova* yourself.
TICKET COLLECTOR	(*laughing*) Beau Brummel!
ALF	Shut up...
TICKET COLLECTOR	Aagh! (*Exits*)

(*Alf puts his feet on the seat in front of him and stares out of the window*)

ALF Blimey, we're actually moving.

(*A well-dressed gentleman enters the compartment. He stops at Alf's legs and looks pointedly at Alf's feet. Else nudges Alf*)

ELSE (*smiling sweetly at gentleman — who is Pakistani*) The gentleman wants to sit down.

(*Alf looks at gentleman. He is unmistakably Pakistani. Pakistani looks at Alf and at Alf's feet — waits patiently. Alf gives in — reluctantly — and removes his feet. The Pakistani pulls out an elegant hankie and dusts seat. He sits down happily*)

ALF Look! (*Sticks his foot under Pakistani's nose*) They're clean, mate.

(*The Pakistani flicks a fag end off sole of Alf's shoe. Alf explodes*)

RITA   Shut up, Dad!

ALF   Probably a bloody sight cleaner than what he is, if the truth's known, eh? (*The Pakistani ignores him. Alf addresses the compartment at large*) If you ask me, old Enoch's right. There'll be a black and white war in 1978. Eh? Don't you reckon?

MIKE   (*embarrassed*) Do you mind?

ALF   No. I don't mind at all. If they want to start on us, mate, they'll get the same as yer bloody Jerry, eh? Don't worry. Blimey, we beat yer bloody Jerry twice — an' he had a bloody good army. (*Chuckles*) But their lot — yer Pakistanis — they couldn't even beat the bloody Indians, an' they're a load of old rubbish, they are. (*The Pakistani remains impassive*) I mean, even that last war they had with each other (*laughs*) — cor, dear, bloody laugh that was. (*The Pakistani does not laugh*) No — they wanna have a go at us. . .what I say — let 'em — any bloody time. Blimey, they don't even know how to keep their flies down. We're bloody fools letting them in in the first place — they stink of curry, all of 'em.

(*The gentleman who has been sitting in the compartment all the time, stares furiously at Alf*)

GENTLEMAN   (*to Pakistani*) Excuse me, sir, but I have been to Pakistan and met your people and (*pointedly at Alf*) I have found them the friendliest, most cultured and sensitive people that it has been my privilege to meet.

PAKISTANI   I do not like Pakistani — especially West Pakistani.

ALF   (*laughing*) Blimey, no pleasing them at all is there? Eh?

(*Ticket collector enters compartment*)

TICKET COLLECTOR   Tickets, please. (*Looks at Alf's tickets*) Sorry, you can't sit in here, not with these tickets. This is first class.

(*It's obviously Alf's fault — the Garnett family has to go*)

ALF   (*pointing to Pakistani*) What about Sambo?

PAKISTANI   (*holds up ticket to ticket collector*) I might be second class citizen, but on British Railways I am first class passenger.

(*Ticket collector clips ticket. Alf is speechless. Ticket collector gestures to Alf to leave. Alf glares through corridor window at Pakistani, who smiles and turns cushion of seat on which Alf has been sitting over to clean side. He then places his own feet on the seat, and turns and smiles at Alf*)

PAKISTANI   Bloody white wog!

(*Alf glares*)

SCENE 3 Bournemouth Central Station: the station cab rank. Alf and family come out of station and go towards cabs. Else and Alf get in taxi.

ALF Commodore Hotel. (*Shuts door*)

MIKE AND RITA Hey — what about us?

ALF Don't be daft — can't all get in 'ere. There's another one behind. See yer down there.

(*Taxi drives off leaving Mike and Rita stranded with baggage*)

SCENE 4 Inside the taxi en route to hotel. Alf looks at watch.

ALF Taking a long time, ain't it. It seems daft building a station out here.

ELSE Never mind — it's a lovely ride. (*Looks out of window*) Oooh look, there's the sea.

ALF (*looks at the sea*) I know it's the sea. What's so special about the sea — I work on the water, don't I?

ELSE It's not the same water at Wapping as you get here.

ALF 'Course it's the same bloody water. It come from here to go to Wapping. See, look, it comes down yer Channel — it passes yer Southampton on yer left — and yer Cowes on your right — up by Dover — and turns left by yer Southend.

ELSE By the Kursaal?

113

ALF	That's right.
ELSE	Where Maud lives.
ALF	I know that — but...
ELSE	She's moving.
ALF	Who is?
ELSE	Maud.
ALF	Look —
ELSE	It's them blacks.
ALF	Look —
ELSE	They've moved in next door to her.
ALF	Will you shut up about your sister Maud!
ELSE	You wouldn't like it if they moved in next door to you.
ALF	No — and if I was a blackie, I wouldn't like it if your sister Maud moved in next door to me neither!
ELSE	Pig!
ALF	Anyway, it's the same water they've got 'ere as we've got in Wapping.
ELSE	So why did we come here for a holiday then? We might just as well have stayed in Wapping.
ALF	Well, I didn't want to come 'ere in the first place, did I?

(*Pause*)

CAB DRIVER	That's the trouble with Bournemouth.
ALF	Wot?
CAB DRIVER	Too many Jews — full of Jews, it is. We've got more Jews here than they've got in Israel — *and* they're more trouble. (*Points*) Another Jewish hotel there — got its own private Jewish beach. They paddle there with their yamelkes on.
ALF	Wot?
CAB DRIVER	You know — the skull caps — them little round hats.
ELSE	(*nudges Alf*) *You* know.

(*Alf glares at her*)

CAB DRIVER	Marvellous business men, them Rabbis — buy chickens at the Cash and Carry. Put kosher stamps on 'em and charge ten pence a pound extra. Very expensive being a Jew, particularly if you're orthodox...

(*Taxi pulls up at hotel*)

SCENE 5 Exterior of hotel. Alf and Else get out of cab. Cab driver does a double take.

CAB DRIVER	(*very embarrassed*) Sorry guv — didn't realise you was Jewish.
ALF	I ain't bloody Jewish!
CAB DRIVER	(*to Else*) 'He ain't bloody Jewish' — who's he kidding? (*Alf reacts*) One seventy-five...(*Alf pays him exactly and stalks off towards hotel*) Hoi! Ikey! (*Alf turns and glares*) Yer bloody Arabs are better tippers!

(*Alf fumes — goes into hotel foyer*)

SCENE 6 Interior of hotel. Rita and Mike are sitting having afternoon tea. Alf and Else enter — they look around.

MIKE	Where have you been?
ALF	Getting here. Where d'you think I've been?
MIKE	Blimey, we've been here a long time. This is our second pot of tea. You don't need a cab here anyway — the station's only round the corner.
ALF	That bloody Jew!
RITA	Dad!

(*Else looks round the room*)

ELSE	Nice, annit? (*Sits down*)
ALF	(*goes to TV*) See we've got a telly...

(*Fat woman enters lounge*)

FAT WOMAN	Don't touch that!

ALF	Eh?
FAT WOMAN	Can't you read? There's no one to touch the television except the proprietors. If you want it on you ask at the desk or ring that bell.

(*She waddles out of room. Alf waits until she has gone and then rings bell. The fat woman reappears*)

FAT WOMAN	D'you ring?
ALF	Yer. I want the telly on.
FAT WOMAN	Well, why didn't you ask me when I was in here before?
ALF	I didn't want it on then.

(*She puts the television on and leaves the room. Alf rings the bell again. Fat woman re-enters*)

ALF	(*giggling*) I want the other channel.
FAT WOMAN	I wish you'd make up your mind!
ELSE	I'm going out.
ALF	Eh?
ELSE	I didn't come to Bournemouth just to sit and watch television — if you did.
ALF	Oh, don't be a spoilsport! (*Else leaves room, followed by Rita and Mike. Alf goes after them. To Mike*) Hey, there's a bar here...

(*Alf and Mike go to bar*)

FAT WOMAN	(*from top of stairs*) It's not open yet.
ALF	It's half past five.
FAT WOMAN	We don't open till six here.
ALF	Annit bloody marvellous?

SCENE 7   Interior of hotel — early evening. Else and Rita sit at bar having a drink. The fat woman and her thin scrawny husband — Harold — are behind the bar.

FAT WOMAN   (*fondling poodle and indicating Harold*) He knows what he wants. He told me straight off, he did — I want something large, he said, not little. He wants me like I am, he said. He won't let me slim. He won't let me take a pound off. He'd leave me if I did. I suppose most men are the same — they like something to get hold of. They like a woman to be a woman not like that Twiggy. Poor girl — most sexless thing. I said to him one day — for a laugh, — I said to him. How would you like to be married to that? Have to go to bed with someone like her? (*She smiles and preens*) He didn't look too pleased. (*Confidentially*) He won't leave me alone, you know. He gets terribly jealous of Poochy. I let her sleep between us, you see. Some nights he starts and Poochy snaps at him. That dampens his ardour. Well, there are some nights when you want to be left alone, aren't there? You know. . .(*Else nods*) Has your husband gone out, Mrs Garnett?

ELSE   Yes.

FAT WOMAN   Oh, I don't let my Harold wander. Well, there's so much for him to do here, you see. There's the cooking an' cleaning. . .all the beds to make. . . It's a long day, running a hotel, and we've got no staff to speak of. And I can't really help. It's a blood thing I've got. I look at him working some days, and I really wish I could be of use — but I daren't lift a finger. He has one afternoon off a week from two till four — I insist on that. Well, all work and no play makes Jack a dull boy.

RITA   I think I'll take the baby up.

(*Rita picks up baby, but is stopped by fat woman*)

FAT WOMAN   Ah, he's asleep. Little dear! (*The dog sees baby and yaps nastily at it. It wakes the baby, who starts to cry*) Oh dear, that's why we're not too keen on young children. They can be so distracting to the other guests. (*The poodle is still yapping. Fat woman glares at baby*) Oh dear, he's upsetting poor little Poochy too. (*To poodle*) There, there — naughty baby, ent he? Yes, I know — mmm. (*Gives dog drinkies of gin*)

SCENE 8   Bar and hallway of hotel: later that night. Alf and Mike enter. Alf is drunk and is being helped by Mike.

ALF   (*sees Harold helping himself to drink*) Ah! (*Harold starts guiltily*) Get — get us some drinks.

HAROLD   It's a bit late, Mr Garnett.

ALF   Get us some drinks. . . 'Late'! Bloody not late. . .

(*Harold pours out drinks and Alf starts to sing loudly and drunkenly. Fat woman appears at top of stairs in nightdress*)

FAT WOMAN   That's enough of that!

ALF   Eh? What are you. . .eh?

FAT WOMAN   (*to her husband*) Put that drink down, Harold. Drink that and you'll be going walkies all night.

ALF   Shurrup! Let's have a song — fat old bitch. . . (*To Harold*) Tell her to go to bed — go on — belongs to you, dun she?

FAT WOMAN   Harold! Close that bar, at once.

ALF   Eh? Bloody marvellous, annit? Come on holiday. . .an'. . .an' you can't bleeding enjoy yourself. Look, Missis — (*Goes to chase her. Fat woman scuttles back upstairs*) Hoi — fatty! I'm talking to you! (*To Harold*) Is. . .is that. . .your wife? What you marry her for? Harold, darling Harold, isn't it? Don't look like Harold Wilson. . .looks more like Harold Macmillan. Eh? She's bloody ugly. No. . .no offence, but she's. . .ugly. . .bloody ugly. Give us a drink. . .Gawd! (*Grabs Mike*) Shouldn't be allowed, should it?

MIKE   What?

ALF   Ugly — bloody ugly women. You (*to Mike*) you're lucky — lucky. You got. . .you got the most beautiful little girl in the world. . .most. . .most beautiful. (*To Harold*) He — he's got. . .not like you. . .he's got the most beautiful wife in the world. Not like you — you've got (*with his face right in Harold's*) the most ugly, the most fat an' ugly wife in. . .the. . . No offence? But, well, you know. . .you've seen her. Most fat an'. . .most ugly. Not like him — not him though. He's got. . .

MIKE   Yeah, I've got. . .

ALF   You've got. . .

MIKE   The most beautiful wife in the world.

ALF That's right. An' you know why? You know why?

MIKE 'Cos you're her father!

ALF 'At's right. An'. . .an' Mummy is her. . .mother. . .see, it's breeding, good breeding, see. . .good stock. (*To Harold*) But you, you know what you've got? No offence, but (*laughs and burps*) — brrrp — what you got is. . .

HAROLD (*looks apprehensively up stairs*) I know what I've got, Mr Garnett.

ALF Right. No offence, but. . .

HAROLD Look, please, Mr Garnett, I want to go to bed.

ALF (*laughing*) What? Brrp — bed? With. . .? (*Points up stairs*) Brrrp. . . (*Straightens himself up and tries to look dignified*) Sorry. Right — your wife — it's your wife. She might be fat. . .ugly. . .but *right* — is your wife. No offence. . . (*He passes out cold*)

SCENE 9 Hotel foyer: next morning. Alf comes downstairs groaning with a hangover. Poodle starts to yap at him. Alf gives it a kick.

ALF Get off!

(*The poodle runs off yapping as Alf sits at dining table*)

FAT WOMAN (*enters*) What d'you want?

ALF Breakfast.

FAT WOMAN	You're too late. Breakfast finished an hour ago. (*She walks out*)
ALF	(*moans*) Bloody hotel...Gawd, my head... (*Goes to window and sees Mike outside putting on green. Alf opens window as Mike putts ball into hole*)
ALF	(*shouting*) Can't you make less bloody noise? (*Groans again and walks into hallway where he sees Else, Rita and baby*) Where are you going?
ELSE	On the beach.
ALF	I ain't had no breakfast, I ain't.
ELSE	Well, that's your fault, isn't it? You shouldn't go out drinking all night. You might feel like getting up in the morning then.
ALF	Gawd, I feel ill.
ELSE	Serves you right.
ALF	I've been sick.
ELSE	I've got no sympathy.
ALF	You wouldn't care if I was dying, would you?
ELSE	Well...I wouldn't let it spoil my holiday. Come on, Rita, let's go out while its nice.

(*Mike comes in and puts putter away*)

MIKE	Let's go up to the Royal Bath. They've got a swimming pool there.
RITA	But we can't use that — we're not residents.
MIKE	It'll be alright if we buy a few drinks. It's open to non-residents. (*To Alf*) D'you fancy a hair of the dog?
ALF	Yer — anything — get rid of this head.
MIKE	Come on then.

(*All exit*)

SCENE 10 The Royal Bath Hotel swimming pool. Alf and Else sit at table by the pool. Mike and Rita are swimming or lying sun bathing.

ALF See, why it's called yer Royal...yer Royal Bath, is in case yer Queen was to come here, to Bournemouth. 'Cos if she come here, y'see, or any of yer Royals, this is where she'd stay. See, every town in England got to have a Royal abode — somewhere for her to stay, see, it's in yer Magna Carta, that is. (*During this speech some girls and a man are playing with a beach ball which keeps hitting Alf in the face. The man continually apologises*) Bloody big kid! See, like, she don't stay where the hoi poloi stays. Well, they could stay as well, but they'd have to smarten up though. I mean, wouldn't be as permissive as it is now — have to cover up a bit then, they would — she'd see to that.

(*A kid jumps into pool, splashing Alf. Alf argues with his mother. Kid moves Alf's chair to edge of pool. Alf goes to sit down — and falls backwards into pool*)

ELSE (*laughing*) Can you swim?

ALF That's a fine time to ask! (*Sinks*)

SCENE 11 The Garnetts' living room: a week later at breakfast. Alf's bald head is peeling.

ALF (*feels his head*) Bloody Bournemouth — I got sunstroke.

ELSE You shouldn't have sat in it.

RITA I tried to put stuff on his head.

ALF Not my fault. You don't expect it — sun to come out like that, out of the blue. I mean, all this year it's been cloudy and rainy. Go to Bournemouth — the bloody sun comes out.

ELSE It was nice. Lovely week.

ALF I blame the BBC.

RITA The BBC? What's it got to do with the BBC?

ALF No bloody warning. They give out gale warnings for your shipping. They should put out sun warnings for your holidaymakers. What's for breakfast? (*Else puts a menu on stand in front of him, hotel fashion. Alf looks at it appreciatively*) Oh (*he studies it*) well, I think I'll start with orange juice.

ELSE It's off.

ALF All right, tomato juice then.

ELSE That's off, too.

ALF (*glowering*) I'll have porridge and kippers then.

ELSE They're off.

ALF What's bloody on then?

ELSE Eggs and bacon.

ALF I'll have that then.

ELSE I'm sorry. Breakfast finished an hour ago. (*She takes menu away*)

(*Alf starts to yell. Else barks at him — like Poochy*)

If we want a proper democracy we've got to start shooting a few people...

Till Death Us Do Part: No. 4 (4th Series)

Recording: 20th August 1972

Transmission: 11th October 1972

If we want a proper democracy we've got to start shooting a few people...

SCENE 1   The Garnetts' living-room at breakfast time. Alf sits reading paper. He looks at the other three members of the family.

ALF   There you are (*indicating paper*) — another one gone. Two up, two down just like this (*indicates the room. Else takes tea pot out into kitchen*) Twenty thousand pounds! Marvellous annit, eh? Bloody marvellous! Old Mac was right, see. He said that...Mr Macmillan senior...he said, 'Vote Tory and we'll make you all capitalists...' An' he was right. They've done it. They've only been in two years and already they've made this house worth twenty thousand pounds. I mean, under your Labour it was only worth six hundred pounds, wasn't it? Eh? And you ask me why I vote Tory. Blimey!

MIKE   But that's not a *real* price. That price is inflationary.

ALF   What are you talking about? Not real? 'Course it's bloody real. It's in the paper — Twenty thousand pounds this house is worth.

127

MIKE	On paper. Only on paper.
ALF	Not only on paper. In my bloody pocket if I wanna sell it.
MIKE	Look, if you sold this house for twenty thousand pounds...right?
ALF	Yer.
MIKE	And you bought next door...
ALF	I wouldn't buy next door.
MIKE	But say you did...
ALF	There'd be no point.
MIKE	But if you did...
ALF	But I wouldn't.
MIKE	Gawd! Look, for the sake of argument, you did.
ALF	All right. For the sake of argument, I did.
MIKE	Right. Now...
ALF	Which I wouldn't.
MIKE	Aah! What's the point?
ALF	That's what I'm wondering.
ELSE	(*Enters from kitchen*)
MIKE	Look, the point is...if you bought next door it'd cost you twenty thousand pounds, wouldn't it? 'Cos if *this* house is worth twenty thousand pounds, then next door is worth twenty thousand pounds, annit?
ALF	(*catches Else's eye*) Could be.
MIKE	It's bound to be! They're identical houses. If this house is worth twenty thousand pounds, then the house next door is worth twenty thousand pounds...and the house next door to that. And the one next door to that...and the one next door to that...
ELSE	There isn't one next door to that.
MIKE	Eh?
ELSE	That's where the gap is. Only bomb we had, that was. There was Jews lived next door to where that dropped. (*Indicates Alf*) He reckoned it was them they was after.
RITA	Oh, Gawd!
ALF	Look, yer Germans had their Intelligence...
ELSE	Old Jowitt was pleased about that bomb.
RITA	Jowitt?
ELSE	The corner shop — as pleased as punch, he was.

RITA   Why?

ELSE   It gave him somewhere to park his van.

ALF   I bet that old bomb site's worth a few bob now, eh? Land, annit? An' that's one thing yer scientists...with all their tecknerlogical skills...that's one thing they can't make, annit? An' that's land. An' that's what I'm sitting on. Twenty thousand pounds worth of it.

MIKE   Yeah...and you couldn't even sell it an' buy next door an' show a profit.

ALF   You couldn't even bloody well *buy* next door! And another thing...nor could yer bloody coons or Pakis, 'cos it's too bleeding expensive. An' that's another thing yer Tories have done. Instead of letting yer coons come in an' buy yer houses an' lower yer land values...yer Tories have put yer leases an' land values up, so yer coons can't afford to buy 'em.

MIKE   Nor can anyone else.

RITA   No.

ALF   An' yer Labour Race Relations Board can't do a bloody thing about it.

MIKE   You — you're mad — you're bloody potty!

ALF   Yer, I know. I'm potty alright. I know that. I've got to be potty to let you live here for the rent you're paying.

RITA   Listen Dad. We pay two pounds a week rent here for one room — one titchy little room.

MIKE   *We're* the ones who are potty!

ALF   So you think two pounds a week is too much, do you?

MIKE   Yeah...but we don't mind mucking-in, like.

    (*Rita laughs*)

ALF   Listen, sonny boy. Let me straighten you out a bit on some of your economics...which you seem to be so full of. On the black day you married 'er (*indicates Rita — Mike and Rita giggle — Rita kisses Mike*) an' started paying your two pounds a week rent, this house had a market value of only six hundred pounds. But over the years, this house has risen in value. It now stands me in at a market value of twenty thousand pounds. Whereas, on the other hand, and according to your own darling Harold, your two pounds has gone down to the value of about twenty-five bloody shillings. So now who's bleeding potty?

RITA   So you want us to pay more rent, do you?

ALF   No. Not necessary. But I'd like you to realise that when he moved in here, during the reign of the Labour Government, he was paying two pounds a week for a room in a six hundred pound house. But now, thanks to me — and a Tory Government — he is only paying twenty-five shillings a week for a room in a twenty thousand pound house.

MIKE   So?

ALF   So under us you've *got on*. And I'd just like you to show a little bit of bleeding gratitude, that's all.

MIKE 'Got on'? You're round the bloody twist. This house was a slum when it was built — and it's *still* a bloody slum.

ALF Yer? Well, it's a twenty thousand pound slum now, annit?

MIKE Look, the way we're going at the moment, you're going to be paying a thousand pounds for a loaf of bread soon. But it won't taste any bleeding better, will it?

ELSE It should do, for that money...

MIKE You'll be collecting your wages then in a bloody wheelbarrow, the same as they did in Germany.

ALF Look, no need to bring yer Germans in. We don't wanna hear about them an' what they done. I know we won the war, an' they done better out of losing it...but that's another argument. That's something yer Labour Party would rather not discuss, for obvious reasons.

MIKE *Eh?*

ALF Never mind about '*eh*'. *(To Else)* We won't fall for that one again, don't worry. *(nods sagely)*

MIKE What are you talking about?

ALF Your Labour Party's Working Man's Internationale, that's what I'm talking about. 'Course, it don't suit their book, do it? It don't suit their book that we're getting prosperous at last, do it?

MIKE *(incredulous)* We're getting prosperous? What — *England*?

ALF Yer. That's right. England. In spite of yer Labour betrayal.

MIKE Labour betrayal? What Labour betrayal?

ALF Don't look all bright-eyed and innocent, Shirley Temple. I mean, who gave yer East Germany to yer Russians?

MIKE I don't know. Who did?

ALF Well, it wasn't Churchill, was it?

MIKE I always thought the Russians took it. I always thought they over-run it and captured it during the war.

ALF Yer, that's right. An' who helped 'em? Eh? Who bloody helped 'em? *(Pause)* Attlee!!! That's who it was — little weasel-face Attlee.

ELSE   Attlee wasn't in charge during the war... It was Winston Churchill. He was in charge during the war.

ALF   (*savagely*) I know he was...

ELSE   He used to wear them hats.

ALF   But while...

ELSE   An' talk on the radio.

ALF   I know...but...

ELSE   An' smoke cigars.

ALF   Look...

ELSE   An' put his fingers up (*does V sign*). He used to put 'em round the other way to Hitler. (*Does the rude version at Alf*)

ALF I *know* that... But while Churchill was out fighting the war, out on the Second Front with the troops...God rest his soul...the other one, bloody ferret-face Attlee, was back home here making plans what he was going to do after the war. Seeking out ways to line the Labour Party's pockets with Russian gold. It's a wonder old Winston never tumbled him. But then, Jesus never tumbled Judas till it was too late.

MIKE *(rises and goes into kitchen)* What are you on about?

ALF You know what I'm on about — the sudden affluence of yer Labour Party after the war. I mean, it was obvious. They was all bloody working class, the lot of 'em. And if it hadn't been for Attlee, all they'd have had when the war ended was their demob money and their cloth caps. I mean, it's bloody plain what happened... When Winnie's out in Yalta talking to Stalin in front of everybody, bloody Attlee's round the back flogging East Germany an' India to Molotov.

ELSE No. It was Ghandi he gave India to... He got in a temper, he did, Ghandi. Got into a nice little paddy, he did, an' wouldn't eat...until they gave him

India. (*Indicates the baby upstairs*) Young Michael's like that. If that baby's in a paddy, he won't take his bottle. If there's something he wants, and he can't have it, he won't take his feed...

RITA (*Laughs*)

ALF Look, yer Ghandi was starving before he started his strike, wasn't he? He was a skeleton nearly before he started it. I mean, he only had a bloody loincloth to stand up in.

ELSE He was their leader, though.

ALF Only a religious leader. See, yer Indians, they looked on Ghandi as a sort of Jesus, as a redeemer, 'cos he looked just like Jesus to them.

ELSE Jesus didn't wear glasses.

ALF He wore a loincloth, though, didn't He?

ELSE But Ghandi wore glasses.

ALF I wear bloody glasses.

ELSE You don't look like Jesus either.

ALF Well, Ghandi did!

ELSE You look more like them that killed Him.

ALF (*Could kill her*)

ALF He looked like Jesus to yer Indians 'cos he lived like Jesus...he lived among the poor...like Jesus...and he renounced wealth like Jesus...and all worldly goods...'cos as the Lord Jesus said, it will be easier for a needle to pass through the eye of a camel than for a rich man to enter the Kingdom of Heaven.

MIKE (*strolls up behind Alf*) Well, He wasn't a Tory then, that's for sure.

ALF (*turns to face Mike*) He wasn't one of your bloody Labour lot, neither!

MIKE No, He was probably a bit of a con...'cos His old man's a capitalist, an He? God.

ALF You...BLASPHEMOUS SCOUSE GIT!!!

MIKE Well, He's got to be. He's got to be a capitalist — He owns Heaven.

RITA He owns the world, too, according to the church.

ALF (*crosses to Rita*) He *made* it!

MIKE Yeah...but the Devil's got shares in it. He's got the concession on all the bingo halls, the Bunny Clubs, turf accountants...an' all that.

RITA God's got the churches.

MIKE Yeah, the way property is gazumping, He's got to be well loaded.

ALF You...blasphemous Liverpudlian Socialist ponce! He'll see you burn, don't worry. He'll have you. Jesus might have been a bit soft, dying for

us...an' letting them Jews knock nails in His hands...but His Father ain't! He's no bloody fool. He'll have you. He'll see you get a bloody fork up your backside...a bloody hot one.

MIKE   God? He can't do nothing.

ALF   He'll have you, mate.

MIKE   All right...all right. I'll challenge Him. If there's a God up there, let Him strike me dead in ten seconds from now.

ALF   Don't worry, He will, He'll have you with a bloody great thunderbolt.

MIKE   Right, starting now. (*Looks at watch*) One!

ALF   (*panics*) Not in this house, I ain't insured against acts of God.

MIKE   Two!

ALF   Get out!!

MIKE   Three!

ALF   Out!!!

MIKE   Four! Five! Six!

ELSE   (*over Mike's counting*) Did you pay his policy this week?

RITA   Ssh!

MIKE   Nine! Ten!

(*Nothing happens. Mike smiles, relieved. There is an enormous bang. Mike hastily crosses himself and hurls himself under the table. A motor bike, which has backfired out in the street, roars away. Alf reacts*)

ALF   He nearly had you then, didn't He?

MIKE   No He didn't.

ALF   No?

MIKE   No. (*Shakily lights wrong end of cigarette*)

ALF   (*laughs*) You recanted in time. You got into gear (*crosses himself*) just in time there, so you want to watch before you join up again with your Communist God mockers. Repent ye! Before it is too late! Tried to destroy this country, didn't you? With your bloody strikes and go-slows...an' your bloody connyverings with your bloody East. All out for something for nothing. And you're all too bleeding simple to know how to get it. Yer bloody Irish have sold out to yer bloody Russians, but we won't... Enoch's wrong, having a go at the coons.

MIKE AND RITA   (*astonished*) Oh!!!

ALF   Yes! He ain't seen the real danger. It's not the coons. We don't want 'em over here stinking the country out with their curries, and making a row on their dustbin lids. But they're bloody harmless — not like yer bloody Russian Unions and yer Chinese Take-Aways... Hot-beds of bloody fifth column, they are. But we're on to 'em, don't worry. You'll see...the next time one of them commy shop stewards goes in the nick, he'll rot there. All they organize them bloody strikes for is so that they can get on the bleeding telly. I blame the BBC for encouraging 'em. They'll put anyone on the bloody telly, they will. Rock an' roll vicars...and sex maniacs, an' bloody Irish gunmen. Admit they put stockings over their heads first, but still... They only let the Queen go on for one show at Christmas — I don't know what they've got against that woman. She should have her own series, 'cos she's better'n' Lulu. (*Rita giggles*) Blimey, she's the best thing on at Christmas.

ELSE You're going to be late for work if you don't hurry up.

ALF *(tying his shoe laces)* Work! There'll be no bloody work to go to soon if the unions have their way. Bloody unions! They're the curse of mankind!

RITA They protect our jobs.

ALF Protect our jobs? I like that. Yer dockers' union was trying to take people's jobs away from them the other day. Yer bloody convicts in yer prisons have got unions now, too — and whose jobs are they trying to protect? Eh? I mean, blimey, who's after *their* jobs?

MIKE The prison unions were formed to improve prison conditions.

ALF Yer! They want their bloody wives in there with 'em, that's all...an' complaining about the food...don't like the porridge...ain't enough bloody sugar in it, I s'pose.

MIKE And why shouldn't they complain? They get fed bloody slops!

ALF And why shouldn't they get bloody slops? Prison's supposed to be a bloody deterrent, annit? They ain't supposed to sit about all day scoffing an' shagging! *(Else is shocked)* I mean, blimey, they'll be putting yer Billy Butlin in charge of the prisons soon, and have bloody red-coats for warders! I mean, in the old days they used to put 'em in bloody chains and ship 'em out to the Colonies. But we can't do that now, 'cos your bloody Labour Party gave all the Colonies away. So we have to keep 'em here an' feed 'em out of our taxes. And what if five of *their* ring leaders defy the law, eh? They can't bung them in prison, 'cos they're already in there.

ELSE They'll have to fine their union.

ALF   Don't be so bloody daft. What are they gonna fine them? Eighty gallons of porridge? A hundredweight of hard tack? And another thing, what would your Russians have done, eh? And your Chinese, eh? If five of their dockers had defied their laws, eh? They wouldn't have put them in prison, would they? EH? No. They'd have bloody shot 'em!

MIKE   And I suppose you'd like to see 'em shoot our dockers, eh?

ALF   We wouldn't! That's the trouble with this country. That's our weakness! If we want a proper democracy here, we've got to start shooting a few people...like yer Russians do!

(*Alf crosses to sideboard and picks up lunch box*)

RITA   The Russians don't shoot people.

ALF   Oh, don't they? What about Stalin? He shot enough. Blimey, they almost run out of people when he was in charge.

RITA   You told us he was an American spy.

ALF   (*puts on his jacket*) Who?

RITA   Stalin. You said he lived down the Mile-End Road, and that he was an American spy.

ALF   Look...

ELSE   Perhaps your dad was right. Perhaps that's why he shot all them Russians.

ALF   Look...

ELSE   He was a Jew, wasn't he?

RITA   Who?

ELSE   Stalin.

MIKE   Geroff...

ELSE   Well...Moseley didn't like him, I know that.

ALF Look, Stalin was a Communist...that's why Moseley didn't like him. Moseley didn't like any Russians.

ELSE Why not?

ALF Because they was all Communists, you silly moo. When he tried to march through Cable Street...

ELSE The Czar wasn't a Communist.

ALF Oh, Gawd! I *know* the Czar wasn't a Communist. Nor is the Queen a Communist.

ELSE She couldn't be.

ALF She don't want to be.

ELSE It's against her religion.

ALF You are bloody bright at times, you are. Sometimes your intelligence bloody astounds me.

ELSE Well, it's true.

ALF Look...

ELSE She believes in God.

ALF I know that.

ELSE Communists don't.

ALF Communists don't believe in wealth neither, do they? They don't like people who are rich, do they?

ELSE Stalin was rich.

ALF Gawd!

ELSE An' he was a Communist.

ALF Look...

ELSE So was Kosygin.

ALF Look...

ELSE And they liked *them*.

ALF Look...

ELSE They made *them* leaders.

ALF Look...

ELSE So they do like some people who are rich.

ALF Look!

ELSE But they don't believe in any kind of God.

ALF I'm going to work. (*Slams cup and saucer on table*)

Mean, bound to get taken short during 160 pages

ELSE Pig!

(*Alf goes to the door, returns and crosses to Mike, grabs the newspaper*)

ALF Buy your own bloody paper. (*Exits and slams door*)

SCENE 2 London wharf setting. Alf enters — kicks at rat — sits down and gets his lunch box out. Fat docker enters, puts his lunch on box, and goes over to a crate.

FAT DOCKER (*forcing open crate and pinching tomatoes*) Y'know, there's so much bloody sawdust in them, you can hardly find the tomatoes. It's not fair…(*bites into tomato*) it's cheating. (*Points to crates*) There's s'posed to be twenty pounds of tomatoes in them…but five pounds of it is sawdust. (*Bangs crate shut*) I mean, it's dishonest trading, annit? 'Cos the bloke who buys them ain't gonna get twenty pounds of tomatoes, is he? Eh? I mean, he's gonna be short, an he? So what's he gonna do, eh? He's gonna bung his loss on to the customer, an he? Yer housewife. That's the trouble with society…there's too many after something for nothing. All yer priorities is wrong.

(*George — another docker — has entered and starts to open crate again*)

FAT DOCKER Don't take 'em out of that crate, George, it's a bit light already.

(*George goes to another crate and forces it open*)

GEORGE This bloody one's light, too.

FAT DOCKER (*looking in it*) Blimey, that's nearly all sawdust. (*Examines crate*) That's been opened on the other side, that 'as.

GEORGE It's been bloody packed like it, mate.

FAT DOCKER Bloody marvellous, annit, eh? Where's it from. (*Looks at label*) "Canaries". (*Turns*) That's the bloody Commonwealth for yer. The sooner we get in the Common Market an' jack that lot the better, I reckon. Bloody thieving bastards! Try another one.

(*George opens another crate*)

GEORGE This one ain't too bad.

FAT DOCKER Yer, I know, but it's got more'n its fair share of bleeding sawdust though, annit? Eh?

GEORGE I opened a case of butter the other day and there was about four pounds missing. It wasn't us, it hadn't been opened this side.

FAT DOCKER What — Australian?

GEORGE Yer. (*Exits*)

FAT DOCKER (*starts to unwrap his sandwiches*) Yer, I know… Well, you can't expect any more from yer Australians, I s'pose… I mean, they was bred from criminal classes wan't they? Eh? It's in their blood to be bleedin' light-fingered, I s'pose. (*To Alf*) Give us another one of them tomatoes while the crate's open, will yer, Alf?

(*Alf gives him a tomato and opens his lunch box. He searches in it*)

ALF Oh, Gawd — the bloody silly moo!

FAT DOCKER What's the matter?

ALF She's forgotten to pack me sandwiches. Annit fair — got nothing to eat now — got no bloody lunch.

FAT DOCKER That's a bit rough, Alf. (*Takes a big bite of sandwich and tomato*) You're gonna be hungry later on.

ALF I'm hungry now.

FAT DOCKER (*with mouth full*) You would be. Did you have any breakfast?

ALF Yer.

FAT DOCKER That's alright, ain't too bad then.

ALF You need a bloody lunch an' all.

FAT DOCKER Yer, you need a good lunch. I tell you what, I couldn't last the day without me lunch. (*Takes a big bite*) These are nice. . .ham. D'you like ham?

ALF (*licks his lips*) Yer.

FAT DOCKER You ain't got no religious hang-ups about it, have you?

ALF Eh?

FAT DOCKER Well, some people won't eat ham. I mean, yer Jew, he won't eat it. Nor will your Muslim. . .or yer Mohammed. An' yer Catholic, he won't eat any kind of meat on a Friday. Not the sort of religion that'd suit me. I like me food too much. Religions interfere with a lot of things but I don't think they ought to be allowed to interfere with yer eating. (*Stuffs his mouth with more ham*) I love a bit of pig. . .I've got this butcher. . .always cuts it the way I like. . .quarter inch thick. . .an' plenty of fat. I love a bit of fat. D'you like a bit of fat?

ALF   Well. . .

FAT DOCKER   I do. . .gives it a flavour. (*Picks up another sandwich*) Here. . .

(*Alf reaches for it expectantly. .Fat Docker lifts top slice and shows Alf the meat*)

FAT DOCKER   Look at that. Lovely, annit? See them veins of fat?

ALF   (*hungrily*) Yer.

(*Fat docker puts slice back on sandwich, and places it with the rest*)

FAT DOCKER   Succulent. I like food. Prefer it to anything. See, there's some blokes like booze. . .some like sex. . .with me it's food. That's why I never got married. Well, be another mouth to feed, wouldn't it? Could be worse. . .could have kids. . .be more mouths to feed. (*Shakes his head*) I couldn't make the sacrifice. I know me. I'd resent every mouthful they ate. I'm not greedy, like. I believe that every man should have his fill. But I don't like it if it comes out of my share. See, I almost died during the war, I did. Went down to fifteen stone, with all that rationing. I tell you, I didn't like Hitler any more than anyone else, but I'd have gone over to him if there'd been any more food in it. (*Takes another huge bite*) I can't stand the thought of being hungry. . . Must be rotten, having no lunch. I know how you must feel. Well, I know how I'd feel. Blimey, it makes me feel rotten just looking at you, sitting there with nothing to eat. I wish I could help you, but I just couldn't bring myself to give you any of mine. Nothing personal, Alf. It's just that I've got this thing about food. It's not even me really, I s'pose. It's me metabolism that makes me the person I am. That's why I'm a Socialist I s'pose. 'Course, I believe in getting my share of this national cake. But I go along with you Tories on one thing — once you've got your share, stick to it. (*Takes a huge bite and chews at it furiously*) Gawd! I hate you Tories when I think of all the food you've got. . .of all the grub they're eating. . .an' others not getting a share of it. Bloody roast ducks and pheasants and (*starts to drool at the mouth*) all them lovely cheeses an' things. . . Gawd, they can sit there an' eat. . .an' eat. . .an' eat. . .an' still have plenty more to eat. Lucky sods. . .they can sit there with a vista of piles an' piles of all sorts of food stretching away into the distance before them, an' all they got to do is spend their lives eating their way through it. Blimey, I wish I could win the pools. (*Looks sorrowfully at sandwich*) Oh, look at that!

ALF   What's wrong?

FAT DOCKER   That's the last one, that is.

ALF   You got one more there.

FAT DOCKER   That's for me tea. (*Puts it away. He starts to eat in a melancholy way*) That's the trouble with you Tories — you don't always see eye to eye with

us in the Labour movement, Alf, but look what the sods have done — they've put extra security on all the docks.

ALF   That's to stop the bloody pilfering, that is.

FAT DOCKER   Oh no, it's not, Alf. It's politics. That extra security is political, mate. See, they've tried putting us in jail for political reasons, ain't they? And they've failed. Failed miserably, they have. Now they're gonna try and nick us for criminal reasons. It's the thin edge, annit? Look, all the lads take out of these docks is in lieu of wages, right?

ALF   No! Not right! The stuff they're taking out of these docks...I mean, it's stealing. Blimey, the way they're going on here, they'll have to nail the bloody cranes down soon.

FAT DOCKER   Look, there's nothing goes out of these docks what ain't our just right — an' the guvnors know it. An' starting this extra security is a slight on your docker's character. It's an insult to your unions and the Labour Movement. I mean, they turned old Ginger Johnson over last night...I mean, a more honest man — Christ, that man's not a criminal!

ALF   What are you talking about? They found two cheeses and a side of beef in the boot of his car.

FAT DOCKER   So they say.

ALF   It's true!

FAT DOCKER   All right, so it's true. But that's not the point, is it? They didn't know he had them things until they searched him. See, up until then he was innocent. So why did they do it, eh? 'Cos he's a union member, that's why, and they're still upset about having to let the other five out.

ALF   Look, that five broke the law, too. That's why they went to prison...and they should have bloody left 'em there.

FAT DOCKER	Hm, a very comradely attitude. Look, those five broke the law because the law was a bad law.
ALF	Look, the law's the bloody law, annit? And that's the end of it.
FAT DOCKER	Well, that's where you're wrong, Alf, 'cos that ain't the end of it.
ALF	It would have been, if I was Prime Minister.
FAT DOCKER	Look, Hitler passed a law in Germany, didn't he? Kill the Jews...was that a good law?
ALF	Not for the Jews, no.
FAT DOCKER	Would you have obeyed it?
ALF	Look, Hitler's dead...
FAT DOCKER	And so are a lot of Jews, and so are a lot of Germans who obeyed his law. So you see, Alf, you've got to think twice before you obey laws.
ALF	Yer, and you've got to think twice before you disobey bloody laws with someone like Hitler in charge. I bet them five dockers wouldn't have been so bloody keen to disobey the law if Hitler had been in charge here instead of Heath. They wouldn't have been so keen to be martyrs then, would they? Eh? 'Cos he'd have made 'em bloody martyrs alright, don't worry.

(*Hooter sounds. Alf rises, preparing to resume work. Fat docker stops him*)

FAT DOCKER	It ain't stopped yet. (*Looking up at sky*) Pity we're not on strike on a day like this. Have you noticed, the last four strikes we've had, it's pissed down. It wouldn't be a bad idea to check the weather reports before they pull us out next time.
ALF	(*reacts miserably*)

SCENE 3   The Garnetts' living-room that evening. Else and the kids watching TV.

ELSE	Well, I don't know how that happened... I cut Michael's. (*To Mike*) I cut yours, didn't I?
MIKE	Yeah.
ELSE	Ham, wasn't it?
MIKE	Yeah.
ELSE	It looked nice, too.
MIKE	Yeah, it was nice.
ALF	I had no bloody lunch, I didn't. He got his, though...bloody marvellous!
ELSE	I'm sorry.
ALF	Yer, I know, I can see you are — bloody moo.
RITA	It's terrible, isn't it?

ALF Yer, it is. Go all bloody day, nothing to eat, just 'cos that silly. . .

RITA I wasn't talking about that. I'm talking about the violence — every time you turn on the television there's riots and industrial violence.

ALF What d'you expect? It's yer bloody summer, annit?

RITA Summer? What's it got to do with summer?

ALF No football.

MIKE Eh?

ALF That's what causes industrial violence.

MIKE It's got nothing to do with football — it's the Government!

ALF Well, that's where you're wrong, annit, clever Dick? See, people need violence, don't they? And when your football's on, they get all the violence they want. . .on the park and off it. But when they take yer football off in summer, they get frustrated an' start riots and industrial violence. 'Cos your cricket's no good. It might be better if they had more body bowling. . .or better still, if they was to let yer bowlers throw the ball at yer batsmen. See, an' then, if he didn't like it, he could run up the pitch and bash the bowler with his bat. I mean, played that way, it might be able to replace yer football. 'Cos it's not enough just to have violence — violence has got to be seen to be done. Anyway (*sits at table*) where's my tea?

ELSE You've had it.

ALF No, I ain't.

ELSE I asked you last night if you wanted the ham for your tea or would you take it with you, and you said you would take it with you.

ALF But I didn't, did I?

ELSE I know.

ALF   Well, where is it?

ELSE   I ate it.

ALF   You ate it!

ELSE   Well, someone had to eat it. Couldn't let it go to waste — that was 60p a pound. Worth it though — very nice.

ALF   You rotten, greedy pig!

ELSE   Right! That's the last time I buy you ham. (*Crosses to armchair and sits*)

ALF   I'm going up the pub!

MIKE   (*rises and crosses to Alf*) Hang on, I'll come with you.

ALF   (*spins round*) You got any money?

MIKE   Well, I was hoping that you might. . .

ALF   Oh no. I've learnt a little lesson from your Socialist lot today. . .your share and share alike mob. What you've got, bloody keep for yourself! (*Exits, slamming door*)

Royal Variety Performance 1972

Recording: 30th October 1972

Transmission: 30th October 1972

from the London Palladium

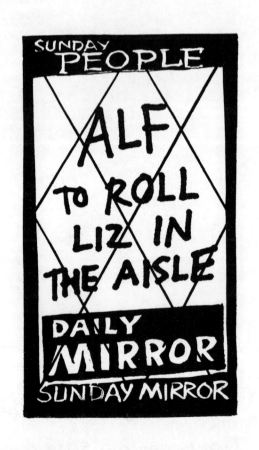

Royal Variety Performance 1972

THE CURTAIN RISES TO REVEAL –

SCENE 1   The Garnetts' living-room. The family sit intently watching the TV.

ALF   (*reading Radio Times*) They ain't got much on there for Her Majesty tonight, have they – on the Royal Command?

ELSE   No. They ain't even got Max Bygraves on this year, either.

ALF   (*looking at Radio Times*) You sure? Blimey, that's strange. They always have him on there. I mean, blimey, Max Bygraves has done more of them Royal Command Shows than the Queen has. I mean, he was doing 'em when her Dad was on the throne. And that's going back a few years.

ELSE   Well, perhaps he's too old to do 'em now.

ALF Who? Max Bygraves? No. He's no older than the Queen Mum is — can't be. Anyway, if they can drag her out, they can drag *him* out. Gawd! Look who they've got on — Jack Jones. That's just a sop to yer trade unions, annit?

RITA (*laughs*) The *singer* Jack Jones.

ALF What's he gonna sing? 'Red Flag'?

RITA Oh, shut up.

ALF Never mind 'shut up'. That's that Lord Hill who's put him on. Boiler Makers' Union, that's how he started, Lord Hill. Now look at him — Head of the BBC.

ELSE No. He was the Radio Doctor.

ALF Who was?

ELSE Lord Hill. He was the first one to swear on the BBC, he was. Always on about opening your bowels, he was.

MIKE Bowels? That's not swearing.

ELSE It's not a very nice word, though, is it?

ALF Look, all that means. . .

ELSE We all know what it means. And I don't think it's very nice to come on the radio and ask everyone if they've opened their bowels yet. (*Points to TV set*) Ooh, look — there's the Queen Mum. She's just arrived. Ah, doesn't she look nice. . . She does look younger than Max Bygraves, doesn't she?

ALF Well

ELSE   Who's that she's with now?

ALF   That's Sir Bernard Delafonte.

MIKE   He's not a Sir.

ALF   An he? Well, I dunno. The way he's all over the Queen Mum there, I bet he's hoping to be. I mean, that's what they're all after. Make out it's for charity, but (*taps his nose*) She knows. Anyway, he's out of luck tonight — she ain't got her sword with her.

ELSE   I hope there's not gonna be any pornography on there tonight — not with her there...

ALF   Don't talk daft. You don't get any pornography on there — not on the telly. Get filth, that's all. The only place you get pornography is in yer Sunday papers.

ELSE I've never seen any...

ALF It's disguised, annit? It's disguised as yer court cases — yer legal proceedings. That case last Sunday — that vicar and the little boy — the reason they took his frock off was —

ELSE We don't want to hear about that!

MIKE Never mind about pornography — you won't even get any swearing on there tonight.

ELSE (*to Mike*) Why not? It's the BBC, annit?

ALF But it's not yer normal BBC tonight. You won't get yer *normal* filth tonight. It's yer *Royal* BBC tonight. They won't let anyone swear on there tonight, not in front of Her. That's why they record it beforehand, see, just in case some foul-mouthed git swears in front of Her. So that if they do, y'see, the BBC can cut it out.

ELSE But if they do swear — she's there — she would hear it anyway...

(*Mike agrees*)

ALF Yer, I know. But that's not the point. (*He rises and goes upstage*) The point is, that She mustn't be seen to have heard it, must She?

MIKE Why not?

ALF (*upstage — turns*) In case it offends *us* — Her loyal subjects!

MIKE It wouldn't offend me.

ALF (*coming downstage*) *Nothing* would offend you, you bloody scouse...

ELSE (*shaking swear-box under Alf's nose*) 10p.

ALF Well... (*Puts money in*)

RITA That swear-box isn't half going to cost you, annit?

ALF Well — bloody thing!

OMNES Ah! Ah! Ah!

ALF (*having to pay up again*) Yer...well, I'll tell you something — if everyone in this country put ten pence in a box every time they swore, we could pay off the National Debt, *and* cure inflation.

RITA You could do it on your own.

ALF (*glares*) Anyway, I bet She wouldn't be bothered if anyone did swear in front of Her, not the Queen Mum. I bet She's used to it. Well, I mean, Philip was in the Navy, wasn't he? An' I bet he lets a few slip now and again. Especially if one of them corgis gets under his feet. Or if he's got a hangover, and that Guards Band starts playing under his window. I bet he gives them a right Royal mouthful.

MIKE Gawd. Yer. Must be awful, that. If you've got a thick head — and all them feet marching up and down outside your window.

ELSE (*to Rita*) It must have been awful for them when the children was young.

RITA What?

ELSE   All that noise. I mean, she might have just got the little ones off to sleep — and then all them soldiers would start, shouting an' hollering, an' banging their drums.

ALF   Yer — be worse than a family of Pakis living next door to you.

RITA   Oh, shut up!

ALF   Must be the same when She's on her boat, with all them sailors coming back off shore leave — I mean, yer Navy's known for its language, annit?

ELSE   I wouldn't fancy that. Having to sleep on the same boat as a lot of drunken sailors.

ALF   Look, I mean, the Queen ain't like you — She's been trained, She know how to handle herself.

ELSE   (*stuffing chocolates*) You'd think they'd give her a box of chocolates, wouldn't you?

RITA   Who?

ELSE   *Her* — Her Majesty.

MIKE   They probably have.

ELSE   I can't see her eating 'em.

ALF   Well you don't think She's gonna sit there in the Royal Box in full view an' stuff her mouth full of chocolates, do you? (*Meaningly at Else*) An' rustle papers and make sucking noises and annoy everyone? She's probably got a drink up there, too, I should think.

RITA   (*laughs*) A drink!

ALF Well, why not? She needs something, don't She, to keep her spirits up...watching that lot. Her Equerry probably brought the Royal bottle up for Her. (*Mike and Rita laugh*) Well, I mean, She can't go in the bar with the others, can She? I mean, She'd be signing autographs all night if She did.

MIKE He's probably got a fag going for her, too, behind the curtain — see, when she leans back, like...she's probably having a quick drag and a sip.

(*Rita mimes this idea*)

ALF (*shocked*) Shut up! You never see that woman with a fag in her mouth.

ELSE Nor Him, neither...well, any of 'em.

ALF (*looks at front cover of Radio Times, with pictures of Royal Command cast*) Look at that 'Royal Rib Tickler' — who are they kidding? Scouse git! Never made me laugh with his Diddymen — ought to get his teeth fixed. I wonder who picked all that lot for Her.

MIKE The Right Honourable Edward Heath. (*Mimes Heath's grin*)

ALF Well, if he did, it ain't as bad as some of the shows your darling Harold used to pick for her.

ELSE Don't she pick 'em herself?

ALF 'Couse She don't — silly moo! If She picked them herself — I mean, blimey, She's got better taste than that. In the old days they used to pick 'em. In the old days, with a Royal Command, yer artists were summoned up to the Palace. Yer Monarch didn't have to come out in the cold to see them. It's a liberty, annit? Rain or shine, they drag 'em out of the Palace up to the Palladium, they do. Blimey, when yer First Elizabeth was on the throne, there was none of that then, mate. She used to summon them up to the Palace, and if they didn't please her, it was chop! — off with their heads!

ELSE   Oh, shut up! (*Indicates TV*) I want to look.

ALF   It's all right when *you* want to talk, isn't it? They ought to let yer Royals run things now, I reckon. Make Prince Philip Prime Minister. (*Mike and Rita laugh*) It'd be cheaper for us, too, if we had him as Prime Minister. I mean, he wouldn't have to have his hand always in he till for a start-off. He's got his own money An' we could flog Downing Street an' Chequers. I mean, Philip wouldn't need them. He's got a better place of his own. I mean, your Buckingham Palace is an altogether more desirable residence than Number Ten, annit?

RITA   (*giggles*) Well, it's detached, isn't it?

ALF   Yes, it is. *And* he wouldn't need that copper on his doorstep either — 'cos he's already got the Army on his.

ELSE   (*trying to watch TV*) Oh shut up!

ALF   And he wouldn't have to waste time, like other ministers, seeking an audience with her, would he? 'Cos he can speak to her any time he wants to, which is his marital rights as her husband. I mean, he could knock off from the House of Commons at night an' sort out all the country's problems with her over a cup of cocoa in bed. I mean, they do most of the Government's work now, anyway. That woman travels the world for us, she does. I mean, look at her last week. Behind the Iron Curtain, She was — up Yugoslavia sorting out yer Bolsheviks — Tito and his mob.

RITA   (*looks at Mike*) Well, at least she gets out! She's the only woman in the country with real Women's Lib.

ALF   What are you talking about?

ELSE   (*to Alf*) When *She* wants to watch television and *She* tells her husband to shut up — he shuts up!

ALF   Well, He ain't married to a great pudden like you!!

ELSE   Pig!

ALF   He's married to a woman who works Her fingers to the bone for us, while Heath — that grammar school twit — is down at Broadstairs getting his bottom scraped.

ELSE   I wish you'd go up the pub.

ALF   I can't go up the pub, can I? I ain't got no money, have I?

ELSE   Oh, take the bloody swear-box! (*Realises what she's said*)

MIKE AND RITA	Mum!!

(*Alf picks up swear-box – sticks it under Else's nose – she has to put her 10p. in*)

ELSE	Pig!
ALF	(*crossing upstage of settee, rattling swear-box at Mike and Rita*) Anybody else? Anybody else? (*To Mike*) You got anything you'd like to say to your father-in-law, Shirley Temple? All contributions gratefully received.

(*Mike puts coins in swear-box, beckons Alf and whispers in his ear – obviously something quite terrible to judge by Alf's expression*)

ALF	(*unable to swear back*) You – you – you!!!

CURTAIN

We are told that when
Jehovah created the world
he saw that it was good.
What would he say now?

George Bernard Shaw